Bible Research

KEN MALMIN

CityChristian Publishing

www.CityChristianPublishing.com

BIBLE RESEARCH

Developing your ability to study the scriptures

BIBLE RESEARCH

Revised Edition
1990

By Ken Malmin

With   Kevin Conner
        Rick Johnston
        Bill Scheidler
        Bob Stricker
        Lanny Hubbard

Published by City Christian Publishing
9200 NE Fremont
Portland, Oregon 97220

Printed in U.S.A.

City Christian Publishing is a ministry of City Bible Church, and is dedicated to serving the local church and its leaders through the production and distribution of quality materials.

It is our prayer that these materials, proven in the context of the local church, will equip leaders in exalting the Lord and extending His kingdom.

For a free catalog of additional resources from City Christian Publishing please call 1-800-777-6057 or visit our web site at www.citychristianpublishing.com.

Bible Research - Revised Edition
© Copyright 1976 by Ken Malmin

Cover design by www.designpointinc.com

ISBN 978-0-914936-71-8

CONTENTS

ACKNOWLEDGMENTS

I would like to acknowledge Lanny Hubbard, Rick Johnston, Bill Scheidler and Bob Stricker who were involved at Portland Bible College in developing the original lessons from which this text was re-written.

Special thanks to Kevin Conner for his substantial contribution to the original lessons and for his permission to include some material from his updated Australian edition of this text.

HOW TO USE THIS BOOK

Believing that Bible study is an essential foundation to both Christian life and ministry, this text has been designed to assist the Bible student in developing his research skills. It was originally developed for the Bible study skills courses at Portland Bible College (Portland, Oregon, USA) and has since been widely used in Bible Colleges, Sunday School classes and Bible study groups of all kinds. Though there are several advantages to group study, this text has been prepared to be effective for individual study as well.

This workbook is also one of the texts used for the "Key of Knowledge" Seminars designed to assist pastors and ministers increase their abilities in Bible study and sermon preparation.

After three introductory chapters, the text is divided into two main sections: Tools for Research and Methods of Research. Both of these sections will include explanations as well as programmed workshop assignments. The assignments are an integral part of the instruction and each should be completed before moving on to a new area. In the "tools" section a group of reference books are dealt with. These study aids have been selected as being basic to Bible study and as representing major areas of Bible research. The design, purpose, and use of each book is explained, followed by its respective workshop assignments. In the "methods" section several ways of studying Scripture are explained and demonstrated. The student will find these to be keys that will unlock the meaning of Scripture to him.

Note to Instructors: This text may be tailored to your needs by omitting or adding certain sections at your discretion. The workshop assignments may be torn out and handed in to you for grading, graded in class or left in the book for grading. Please feel free to communicate with the author concerning the use of this text.

Section I
INTRODUCTION TO RESEARCH

CHAPTER ONE

IMPORTANCE OF STUDYING THE BIBLE

I. **IMPORTANCE OF THE BIBLE**

    A.   **How The Bible Is Superior**

        The Bible far surpasses any other book as to its relevancy and importance to mankind. It is the only book in man's possession written by God and infallibly revealing His will. It is the most reliable means of knowing both God and man.

        The Bible is a source of many things to those who believe. The following is a condensed list of some of these.

1.	Salvation	II Timothy 3:15; James 1:21
2.	Life	John 20:31; Psalm 119:93
3.	Divine Nature	II Peter 2:2
4.	Growth	I Peter 2:2
5.	Sanctification	Psalm 119:9, 11
6.	Peace	Psalm 85:8; 119:165
7.	Joy	Jeremiah 15:16; Ps 1:2
8.	Guidance	Psalm 119:105
9.	Wisdom	Psalm 119:98
10.	Faith	Romans 10:17

        Though not an end in itself, the Bible, as no other book, leads us to a knowledge of God and of all the basic issues of life. It is an invaluable tool to help man fulfill the reason for his existence.

    B.   **How The Bible Meets The Needs Of Mankind**

        1.   Man needs **communication** from God. Sin created a communication gap between God and man. The means that God chose to bridge this communication gap was **THE WORD**. Occultism abounds because man is seeking to bridge the gap between himself and the spirit world. God has already done this in Christ.

        2.   Man needs **revelation**. Man can only know God through God revealing Himself to man. The Lord reveals Himself by His Word (I Samuel 3:21). It is the only tangible infallible revelation given to man from God. It is the mind of God. Creation reveals God's power. The Scriptures reveal God's person and character.

        3.   Man needs **Divine adjustment**.
                II Timothy 3:16. The fourfold use of the words of Scripture:
                a. Doctrine -- Teaching, instruction.

                b. Reproof.

                c. Correction.

d. Instruction.

The purpose is that man may be thoroughly perfected, or adjusted, unto Divine righteousness. Psalm 19:7-9. The end of all Bible study is that man may be conformed to the image and likeness of God in Christ.

4. What Man Is Like Without The Word

Without the Word of God in a person's life, man is likened unto:

a. A man in the darkness without a lighted lamp. Psalm 119:105.
b. A car without a steering wheel -- cannot be driven.
c. A ship without a rudder -- directionless.
d. A boat without a sail -- just drifting.
e. A person without a compass -- lost.
f. A house without a foundation -- unstable and unable to withstand storms.
g. A child without any education -- ignorant.
h. A planet without a sun -- lifeless.
i. A man without a map -- no sense of his position.

Each of these things are a means to an end, not the end in themselves. All are to bring us to the desired destination, to bring us to HIM, John 5:39,40. The Bible explains man's origin, the entrance of sin, the purpose of our existence, the meaning of life and eternal destinies. It cannot be compared with the totality of the books of men.

The Bible is heaven's education and wisdom (I Corinthians chapters 1-2). It is more valuable than all earth's educational courses. It prepares men for earth and heaven, for time and eternity.

The Bible is a means to an end, not the end in itself. Otherwise we can become guilty of worshipping a book instead of the PERSON the book points to.

II. THE IMPORTANCE OF RESEARCH

Realizing the importance of the Bible in the Christian life, it becomes essential that we understand how to use the Bible. Most Christians have understood that they should read, meditate on, memorize, and live the Bible, but now a rapidly increasing number are realizing that to better facilitate all these they must also study the Bible.

The Bible is a book that is at times easy and at other times difficult to understand. Anyone who has read very far in its pages has soon discovered that there are many things that must be interpreted in order to discern their meaning. This is true not only because the Bible is deity speaking to humanity but also because God used human vessels through which to communicate His truth. In many ways He adapted and communicated His message through their own frames of reference. For this reason, study that goes far beyond mere reading is essential to fully understand the Word of God. There is no substitute for diligent Bible study.

Understanding the Bible not only involves substantial effort but also requires having a right heart. A person's attitude toward the Scriptures will determine what he receives from them. All Bible students should cultivate the following attitudes:

A. **Attitude of hunger for the Word** - Proverbs 2:1-11; Psalm 119:20; Job 23:12; Psalm 19:7-10; Ezekiel 3:1-3; Matthew 4:4; Revelation 10:1-10. A passion for the Word is needed.

B. **Attitude of love for the Word** - Psalm 119:47, 97, 113, 119, 127. This comes through knowing its Author.

C. **Attitude of enjoyment of the Word** - 1 Peter 2:2; Ephesians 5:26; Jeremiah 15:16; Psalm 119:16. One learns most what he enjoys the most. Psalm 21:2; 37:4.

D. **Attitude of respect for the Word** - Psalm 119:6, 15.

E. **Attitude of teachableness** - Psalm 119:33-40; Matthew 6:33; Mark 7:7.

F. **Attitude of meekness of spirit** - James 1:21. Humility of mind - Philippians 2:3; Acts 20:19; I Peter 5:5. Pride and arrogance bring spiritual blindness. "A know-it-all" discovers very little Acts 13:27; Isaiah 66:1-5; I Corinthians 1:25-29; Jeremiah 4:22.

G. **Attitude of meditation in the Word** - Psalm 1:2; Joshua 1:8; Psalm 119:48, 78, 148. The Ethiopian eunuch read and pondered the Word and the Lord sent the right ministry at the right time to instruct him. Acts 8:27-40.

H. **Attitude of a worshipful spirit** - Revelation chapters 4-5. The book remained sealed until the worship arose.

I. **Attitude of desiring personal and practical application.** The goal of Bible study and reading should be personal and practical application of the truths to one's daily lifestyle. Our desire should be not just for information, but also for formation of character.

CHAPTER TWO

BRIDGING THE COMMUNICATION GAP

I. BECOMING DIVINE COMMUNICATORS

Beyond personal devotion in one's life there should be another purpose in the study and research of the Word of God, that is, to be a communicator of God's Word. There is no greater calling than to be a skilled communicator of the Divine revelation.

Jeremiah 1:9. God told Jeremiah, "I have put MY WORDS in YOUR MOUTH!" The mouth does not originate the words but only speaks them. The mouth is the channel of communication of the thoughts of the mind.

The word originates in God's mind. It is our responsibility to speak with words that God gives thus becoming God's mouthpiece to His people, or mankind.

Jeremiah 15:19. Take the precious from the vile (no mixture of the word), and you shall be as my mouth (mouthpiece).

I Peter 4:11. Speak as the oracles of God. I Kings 6:11-36. The Holiest of All in the Temple was "the oracle" - lit. "The speaking place" of God's voice, from off the blood-stained mercy-seat of the Ark of the Covenant. Believers are to be God's speaking place. His mouthpiece, His oracle.

Acts 10:22; 11:14. Cornelius was to hear words from Peter, whereby he would be saved.

Our purpose and motive in study is to be the best communicators of the Word of God that we can be to please God and to see His Word live in others.

Philemon 6. That the communication of thy faith may become effectual by the acknowledging of every good thing which is in thee in Christ Jesus. When it is effectual it really works. It is real "koinonia", communication, sharing, participation, fellowship of the Word of God. It is communicating our faith to others!

II. CHRISTIAN COMMUNICATION

The following article, by Jay Green, is taken from **The Christian Literature World**, P.O. Box 5103, Marshallton, Delaware, December 1974, Number 9:

CHRISTIAN COMMUNICATION

In an age where Christian values can be plainly seen vanishing from both public and private lives, the communication of the good news about Jesus Christ becomes a must if we are to avoid the repetition of the dark ages.

Alas! Hardly anyone is giving any attention to defining communication, much less to refining their own ability to communicate the Gospel and all its wonders. As a starter toward your personal study of this art, please accept the following pointers. You, too, can be a master communicator -- all you need to do is to try hard to become one of those who has organized himself and his message to be God's tools in turning the world back right-side up.

WHAT COMMUNICATION IS

The dictionary definition of communication is, in part, (a) the act of imparting or bestowing; (b) the act of sharing or participating; (c) the interchange of thoughts or opinions by speech or writing, etc. This, in brief, means that to communicate, one must send a message which will be received. If the message is not received, therefore, you have not successfully communicated. It is not enough to place the blame on the receiver, for it is the responsibility of the communicator to see that his message is received.

WHAT IT IS TO SEND

A message cannot be said to be sent unless it obeys the fundamental rules of communication.

1. The sender must know the nature of the recipient, how he thinks and reacts, what he likes, and particularly what he dislikes. It is said of Aristotle that "he sought (his principles) in the living pattern of the human heart, all the recesses and windings of that hidden region he has explored; all its caprices and affections, whatever tends to excite, ruffle, amuse, gratify, or to offend it, have been carefully examined..." - Copleston, **A Reply to the Calumnies of the Edinburgh Review Against Oxford**, 1810, p. 26.

2. The sender must have a definite purpose, that of transferring a central idea or theme. Usually this will be done by stating a proposition, then presenting it.

3. The sender must select pertinent, adequate and efficient materials in order to arrest the attention of the recipient, gain his assent, and in order to produce the desired reaction.

4. This requires that the sender organize the material sent on a definite pattern, using methods that are best fitted for the purpose.

5. This also requires that the sender have a thorough knowledge of words, their meaning, their connotations, their force, etc. It is important that he know what they mean to the one he addresses.

6. Lastly, a message cannot be said to be sent unless it is sent in a fashion acceptable to the recipient.

[The above rules and other useful information available in **Fundamentals of Communication**, Wayne Thompson.]

WHAT A MESSAGE IS

In communication, the message is that thought, idea, theme, or proposition which the sender intends to impart to the recipient. It will not be a proper message unless it conveys the thought of the sender in its entirety. Therefore, the message must be given in words that exactly transfer the meaning of the sender to the recipient. The message will be defective if it does not fulfill the intention of the sender.

WHAT RECEIVING IS

A communication is not received, then, unless the recipient knows and understands the thought or idea intended by the sender. You have not communicated unless your idea is transferred to the recipient. Usually receiving is accompanied by some acknowledgment of the message, such as a corresponding action which can be traced to the message. This could take the form of (1) a readjustment of the thinking of the recipient, or (2) a return message for clarification, or for further information, or for additional motivation; or (3) an action which can be seen to be based on the content of the message.

In summary, at the very least a true communication is one that has been properly prepared and sent so as to succeed in informing, enlightening, and/or motivating the receiver of it.

CHRISTIAN COMMUNICATION

While the rules of communication strictly apply, it still must be recognized that Christian communication differs from all other types of communication. It is different in its aim, in its message, in the originator of its message, and in its desired result.

1. The AIM of Christian communication is to convey God's thoughts to your intended recipient. In this the Christian is only a vessel in which God's message is carried. The Word of God is perfect. It is the ultimate communication to man, being prepared specifically by the Creator for the benefit of the creatures He has chosen to be partakers of the divine nature. Since a Christian is also a sinner, it is obvious that the pure message from God can be contaminated by Human carriers. Therefore, if we as Christians desire to fulfill the aim of Christian communication, we must be aware of our uncleanness, we must purify ourselves, being

cleansed from our natural thoughts and purposes. In this way only may we be vessels fitted for the Master's use in conveying His message of good news regarding Jesus Christ.

2. The MESSAGE in Christian communication is the Word of God as solely contained and encompassed in the Bible: **"All Scripture is God-breathed and profitable for teaching, for reproof, for correction, for instruction in righteousness; so that the man of God may be perfect, fully fitted unto all good works"** -- II Timothy 3:16,17. We then must recognize that:

(a) The all-wise God has exactly and precisely prepared the Scriptures as His message to all sorts, kinds and races of men everywhere. Not one jot nor one tittle needs to be added to the written Word, nor may anything be subtracted from it as an accommodation to the understanding of man. This is quite different from normal communication between men, where one may trim the message, or expand the message, etc. in order to convey one's idea or them. Whoever adds to God's message, or subtracts from it, is in danger of hellfire, his place in the Book of Life evidenced by such action (Revelation 22:19).

(b) Being the ultimate message, and being filled with things that are **'hard to understand which the ignorant and unsettled ones pervert"** (II Peter 3:16), God gives His servants the privilege and the solemn responsibility to read in the Book clearly, and to give the sense and to cause the receiver to understand (see Nehemiah 8:8).

The RESULT of communication of the Christian message is the fulfillment of the plan of God in the life of the person receiving it. God's Word never returns to Him void. It is either a savor of life unto life, or a savor of death unto death. In all cases, it accomplishes God's purpose. This does not relieve us as communicators of God's message from the responsibility that results from slothful communication. It is a shame and a disgrace for a Christian to lightly receive, and unskillfully discharge his responsibility to communicate the Gospel to those within his reach.

It should be kept in mind that no Christian communication is possible unless we as carriers intend that God's will and judgment be conveyed to the recipient. Any attempt to interpose ourselves and our own interpretations as standards of belief will cause the communication to be defective. And it will be defective in the degree that we selfishly interject our own ideas and purposes. It was written of John Calvin that, "he labored to declare not his own mind, but the mind of the Spirit as couched in (Scripture)" -- C.H. Spurgeon, **Commenting and Commentaries**.

COMMUNICATING GOD'S MESSAGE IN WRITING

It pleased God, after some thousands of years of oral communication, to commit His message to writing. He had by then proud that it was not impossible for Him to maintain a pure and unadulterated message, even when the only conveyance used was the mind and speech of sinful man. Yet, man being only evil continually (Genesis 6:5), and God intending the communication of a far deeper knowledge of Himself as His purpose and plan unfolded providentially. He implemented His plan to expand His word to men and to record it in writing.

This not only formed the basis for the fullest understanding by men in this world, but also was to state unequivocally and fully the standard by which all men are to be judged in that Day (John 12:48). Furthermore, this written Word is the sole basis for that which will be taught to God's elect people throughout all eternity.

Having been designed, then, to be the standard by which all men were to be judged, and the basis for all future instruction to men, God constructed the Word so as to leave us without any excuse either in believing it, or in receiving it, or in transmitting it. As such, Christians can confidently transmit and communicate the Word of God with the greatest fidelity. Remembering that **'the Word of God is living and powerful and sharper than any two-edged sword, piercing even to the dividing apart of both soul and spirit, and both the joints and marrow; and a judge of the thoughts and intentions of the heart"** (Hebrews 4:12), we must lovingly, carefully, tenderly prepare and present God's message so as to implant it whole and unadulterated in the mind of those who read or hear it from us.

SUCCESSFUL CHRISTIAN COMMUNICATION

Words fitly framed together are like apples of gold, etc. Words spoken have turned the world upside down (Acts 17:6). Words written have, however, the advantage of a more precise presentation of the message. That which the apostle Paul spoke to the Ephesians, for example, was no sublime speech, but that which he wrote with his pen to the Ephesians is enshrined in our hearts forever and forever as God's perfect communication.

If we are to successfully communicate God's message, at least these four things should be a part of our planning and prayerful preparation:

1. That which we present must be full of life, spirit and fire: **"It is the Spirit that makes alive; the flesh profits nothing. The words that I speak to you are spirit and life"** (John 6:63). **"He that believes on me...out of his belly shall flow rivers of living water"** (John 7:38). **"For coming to Him a living Stone, indeed rejected by men, but chosen by God, and precious, you also as living stones are built up a spiritual house, a holy priesthood, to offer up spiritual sacrifices acceptable to God by Jesus Christ"** (I Peter 2:4). **"Which things we also speak, not in the words which man's wisdom teaches, but in the words the Holy Spirit teaches, explaining spiritual things by spiritual means"** (I Corinthians 2:13).

God alone can put fire in your communication: **"I will make My words in your mouth fire, and will make this people wood, and it shall devour them"** (Jeremiah 5:14). **"But His Word was in my heart like a burning fire shut up in my bones, and I was weary, with holding in, and I could not stop"** (Jeremiah 20:9). What God did for Jeremiah in a time of destruction, He does for His communicators in times of construction. What else but godly fire came out of the mouths of Peter and Paul as literally thousands turned to God in one day?

2. Our message must be solidly based on Scripture, being no more than an honest expounding of God's message, **"not in words which man's wisdom teaches, but in the words the Holy Spirit teaches"** (I Corinthians 2:13) -- **"For the weapons of our warfare are not fleshly, but mighty through God, to the pulling down of strongholds, overthrowing imaginations and every high thing lifting up against the knowledge of God, and bringing into captivity every thought into obedience of Christ"** (II Corinthians 10:4,5).

3. It must be prayerfully related to the heart and conscience of the recipient. The sense must be plainly given, distinctly enunciated in words we have reason to believe will be understood, and repeated as often as is necessary for the successful communication of the message. Personal application is essential (**"to the Jews I am a Jew, etc."**) and the better the writer, the more apt he becomes in tailoring his points into fishhooks that implant themselves in the inner being of the recipient, never to be torn out and easily forgotten.

4. God's message is our message; a message of peace and restoration, a message of mercy and love, therefore it must be communicated by one with love unfeigned, faith unpretended, and humility undeniable.

Be exhorted then to become active and successful communicators of God's message. His written Word regarding the living Word, the Savior and Lord to whom all must look for deliverance. And at the very same time, be exhorted to be active and persistent receivers of God's message. You can't communicate, for instance, if you do not yourself hear and incorporate God's message into your own life and being. To this end, you must attend to the many communications God has given to you by the great Christian writers God is now raising up to couch His message in the words that you have learned to understand. Who is to say that there is not yet left in God's quiver an Augustine, a Luther, a Calvin, a Bunyan, a Goodwin, an Owen, an Edwards, an Alleine, a Spurgeon, a Kuyper, a crystal-clear Bonar? You yourself may be one like these.

--Jay Green

III. THE COMMUNICATION OF SCRIPTURE

A. Communication In Creation – Before Sin

1. In the creation of man, God made man in His own image to have full fellowship with Him and bring man into His full purpose (Genesis 1:27-31).

2. Man's spirit, mind, and intelligence was unhindered in its operation (Genesis 2:19,20).

3. Before the entrance of sin, man had unbroken communication with God. Genesis 3:8. The experience which follows intimates undoubtedly what Adam had with God before sin came in. This communication between God and man is symbolized in the expression "open heavens."

   a. Moses and the elders "saw God...the body of heaven..." (Exodus 24:9-11).

   b. Ezekiel had "open heavens" (Ezekiel 1:1).

   c. Jesus also had "open heavens" (Matthew 3:16; Mark 1:10; Luke 3:21).

   Note also these Scriptures: John 1:51; Acts 7:56; 10:11; II Corinthians 12:1-4; Revelation 4:1; 11:19; 15:5; 19:11.

Thus there was not a communication gap before the entrance of sin.

B. Communication Gap Between God and Man - After Sin

The moment man sinned, there came about a communication gap between God and man. SIN brings a communication gap, a communication breakdown between Creature and Creator (Genesis 3:1-24). Thus instead of "open heavens", the heavens became as brass and iron on earth (Deuteronomy 28:23; Leviticus 26:19; I Kings 8:35-36). Heaven was shut against man. There was a great gulf fixed.

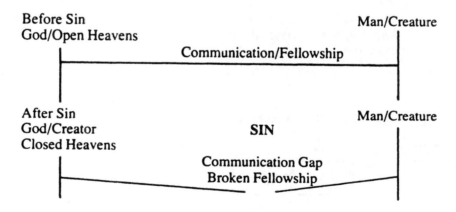

Before Sin
God/Open Heavens   Man/Creature

Communication/Fellowship

After Sin
God/Creator   SIN   Man/Creature
Closed Heavens

Communication Gap
Broken Fellowship

Who can bridge this gap? How can it be bridged? The world of the occult and Satan-worship are evidences of man's attempt to bridge this communication-gap between the spirit realm, the supernatural and the natural realms. However, only GOD can bridge this great gulf fixed (Luke 16:19-26). This He has done in the Bible and in Christ.

C.   **Communication Gap Bridged** - Grace of God

God comes in grace to Adam to bridge the gap that had come because of sin. It is God who takes the initiative.
Man is uncovered, clothed with guilt, hiding from the presence of the Lord, and trying to balance out the guilt and the blame.
God brings in a substitutionary sacrifice, clothing Adam and Eve with the coats of skin, restoring communication and fellowship through the blood. There at Eden's gate He placed the cherubim and the flaming sword and His Shekinah glory, and there in the cool of the evening He would fellowship with man.
In due time God gave Israel the Tabernacle with its Ark of the Covenant, and from the blood-stained mercy seat and Cherubim He communicated with man by the High Priest, Aaron (Exodus 25:10-22).
"There I will meet with you, there I will **commune** with you, from above the mercy seat."
Read also Numbers 7:89, Genesis 18:33; Exodus 31:18. God communed with His own.
The thing that God used to bridge the communication gap was the blood of atonement. On this foundation alone, communication was re-established. Apart from blood atonement, the blood of Jesus, God has nothing to say to fallen man, except in judgment (Hebrews 10:22; Matthew 26:26-28; Hebrews 12:24). The blood speaks to God. Hence when men reject the blood of Jesus Christ, God's sacrifice for sin, they cannot have fellowship with God or commune with Him. They are rejecting God's bridge, in Christ, through the cross. (Refer to Hebrews 1:1-2, Amplified New Testament, and 'Interpreting the Scriptures" for about twenty ways in which God communicated to man, pp. 8,9,10).

D.   **Communication of the Scripture** - The Holy Bible

The greatest communication of God to man is in THE SCRIPTURES, the Holy Bible. God spoke His Word (John 17:17; II Timothy 3:16). We have revelation and inspiration and the result is the infallible Scripture. God did not use a universal tape-recorder, nor angels to write Scripture or preach the Gospel. He used about forty different writers to write His Word.
The Bible is God's communication to Man. Forty different writers, yet one Author.
The diagram illustrates the process of communication of the Scriptures from God through man to man.

THE COMMUNICATION OF SCRIPTURE

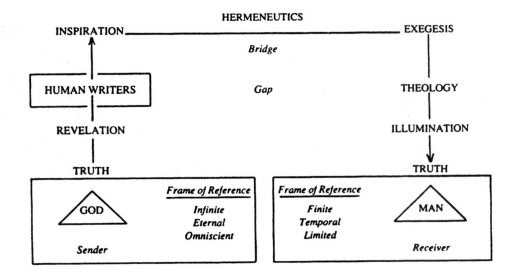

10

Thus we have:

God -   The Sender, the communicator.
               His frame of reference is infinite, eternal, omniscient, all truth.

Man -   The receiver, the communicatee.
               His frame of reference is finite, temporal, limited. In this case, the writers
               of the Scripture receive truth from God.

Bridge -   The communication gap has to be bridged between God and man, and
               now man and man. This is hermeneutics, or principles of interpreting the
               Scriptures.

Hermeneutics then is the science and art of interpretation, interpreting the Bible, God's
communication to man.
God bridged this gap between Himself and the writers of Divine revelation in various ways
that He spoke to them.
Now the next bridge has to be built between the writers of Scripture and their and our
generation.

IV.   BUILDING BRIDGES

The diagram here illustrates the next bridge that has to be built between the writers of Scripture and
their and our generation, which also has to follow in our communication of the Gospel to the
unbeliever.

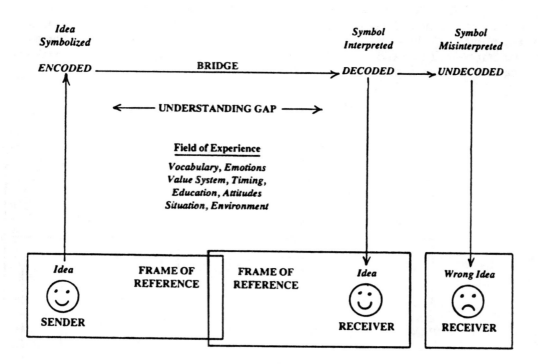

Thus we have here:

Writer - The Sender to their and our generation. Communicator. Frame of reference. Idea symbolized. Message encoded.

Believer - The receiver. Communicatee. Symbol interpreted. Idea decoded. Frame of reference difference.

Unbeliever - The receiver. The believer has now to bridge the gap between himself and the unbeliever's frame of reference.
If not understood, symbol misinterpreted, undecoded, gets the wrong idea, then the believer has not communicated the message.

In each of the above, all have their own field of experience, i.e., vocabulary, emotions, value system, timing, education, attitudes, situation, environment, etc.

This extends to teacher and student; minister and congregation; saint and sinner. All have to bridge the communication gap brought about by sin. This is especially so when it comes to redeemed sinners, yet imperfect, and the communication of the Divine communication to unredeemed sinners. God sees all; man has limited frame of reference. God sees beginning and end and all in between. Man sees neither beginning nor end often, but the limited present with his limited frame of reference.

V. THE FOUR GAPS TO BE BRIDGED

As already noted, inseparably connected with Principles of Bible Research are the Principles of Biblical Interpretation, or Hermeneutics.

The goal of hermeneutics is to properly determine what God has said in the Scriptures; to determine the meaning of the Word of God. The foundation for reaching this objective is the bridging of the understanding gap is the foundational **means** for reaching the desired **end**; knowing what God meant by what He said. This gap is basically fourfold: the linguistic gap, the cultural gap, the geographical gap, and the historical gap. Each of these will be considered using a problem/solution approach.

BUILDING THE BRIDGE

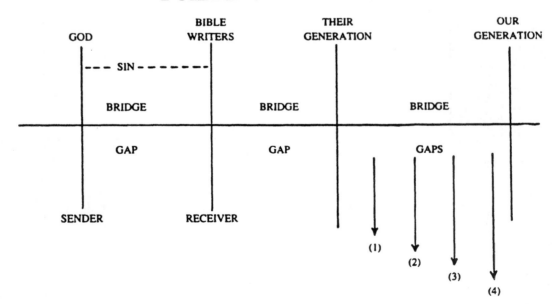

A. **The Linguistic Gap**

1. **Problem**: The Bible was written in three languages which are no longer in use. Ancient Hebrew, Ancient Chaldee and Koine Greek have long been extinct as spoken languages.

2. **Solution**: The way to bridge this linguistic gap is to study linguistics. Webster's dictionary defines linguistics as: "The science of languages; the origin, signification, and application of words; also called comparative philology." It is necessary to study Ancient Hebrew, Ancient Chaldee and Koine Greek in order to be able to read and understand the earliest Biblical manuscripts. This involves study in three basic areas: vocabulary, grammar and genre.

   a. **Vocabulary**: In order to understand a sentence, it is necessary to understand the words of which that sentence is composed. There are four approaches to accomplishing this task;

      (1). The **Etymological** study of a word - attempting to understand a word by examining its origin, derivation, formation and history (e.g., the Greek word for obedience, HUPAKOE, comes from two Greek words: HUPO, which means "under"; and AKOUO, which means "to hear." Thus obedience is a "hearing under").

      (2). The **Comparative** study of a word - attempting to understand a word by studying all of its occurrences in Scripture. This can be properly done only by taking a Hebrew or Greek word, not just the English equivalent, and noting every usage of it in Scripture (e.g., the Greek word DIAKRINO is translated in the King James Version: "to discern, to doubt, waver, to be partial, to make a difference").

      (3). The **Cultural** study of a word - attempting to understand a word by ascertaining its original cultural meaning. This involves the literal sense of the word, which is its basic customary and socially designated meaning (e.g., the word "adoption" in modern day culture refers to the transferring of a child from one family to another, but in Hebrew culture it referred to a child coming of age in his own family).

      (4). The study of a word in **Cognate Languages** - attempting to understand a word by investigating its equivalents in related languages (e.g., equivalent words in Aramaic may help to clarify the Hebrew, since the two languages are so closely related).

   b. **Grammar**: In order to understand a sentence it is not only necessary to have defined its words, but it is also essential to understand the part each word plays in the sentence. This leads to a study of the general principles and particular rules for writing the languages of the Bible. The same methods used to research the meanings of the words can also be used to research grammar. The study of vocabulary supplies the parts, while the study of grammar provides the rules for putting the parts together into a whole.

In studying grammar it soon becomes evident that languages are structurally different. In other words, their sentences and paragraphs are put together in different ways. Languages are structured in one of two basic ways, or in a combination of the two.

(1) **Analytic Languages** - These are languages in which the order of the words in a sentence determines the role each word plays in that sentence (e.g., whether a word is a subject, indirect object, or a direct object). Hebrew and English are both analytic languages in that they stress word order.

(2) **Synthetic Languages** - These are languages in which the ending of a word determines the role it plays in the sentence. Greek is a synthetic language stressing word ending (e.g., **anthropos** = a man [subject]; **anthropo** = to a man [indirect object]; **anthropon** = a man [direct object].

In summary, we cannot over emphasize the importance of studying **vocabulary and grammar** together in order to arrive at proper exegesis. Word studies alone are insufficient, apart from grammatical considerations, to bring about correct interpretation.

c. **Genre**: In order to understand a writing, its literary genre (kind or style) must first be determined. It is the genre of the passage or book which sets the mood or stance from which the rest of the passage or book is seen. Literary genre can be illustrated by three concentric circles:

(1) **Literary style** - When a book of the Bible is approached, the first step in interpretation is to determine its literary style (e.g., whether it is historical, poetical, apocalyptical or prophetical).

(2) **Literary expression** - Within any literary style there can occur passages, utilizing unusual forms of literary expression (e.g., parables, allegories, psalms and riddles).

(3) **Figures of speech** - Within any literary style or expression there may occur a figure of speech; that is, a phrase or a sentence in which the author expresses himself using words in a way differing from their normal use (e.g., metaphors, similes and idioms).

Just as vocabulary should not be considered apart from grammar, neither should vocabulary and grammar be considered apart from literary genre in solving the problem of the linguistic gap. The following is a diagram and illustration of the three circles of genre. It should be recognized that the illustration is partially inadequate in that the figures of speech may be found outside of special literary expressions.

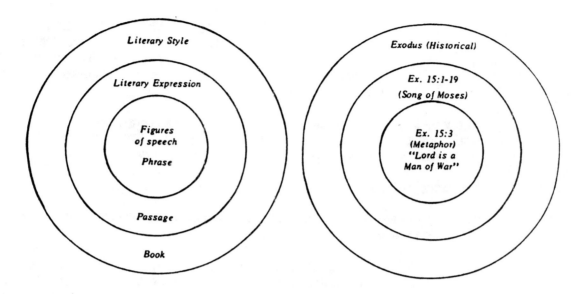

B. The Cultural Gap

1. **Problem**: The cultural contexts of the Biblical writers differ vastly from the cultural context of the modern day reader.

2. **Solution**: The cultural gap may be bridged by studying the cultures in which the writers of Scripture lived. However, the solution to this problem is made more complex by the fact that different writers lived in cultural settings diverse from one another. As the centuries passed, God's people were influenced culturally by the Egyptian, Phoenician, Assyrian, Babylonian, Persian, Grecian and Roman cultures.

   By "culture" we mean the ways and means, both material and social, whereby a given people carry on their existence. The cultural gap in its broadest sense would certainly include the linguistic gap, the historical gap, and the geographical gap. But for the purposes of this outline, we are using it in a much narrower sense. The study of Biblical cultures can be divided into two main classifications:

   a. **Material Culture**: In order to understand a society it is necessary to study the material features and expressions of that society. This includes a consideration of such things as housing, cooking utensils, food, clothing, agricultural implements, weapons, means of transportation, animals, art forms and religious articles (e.g., it is impossible to properly interpret Jeremiah 2:13 without an understanding of what a "cistern" represented in that cultural context).

   b. **Social Culture**: In order to understand a society it is also necessary to explore the way things are done and the manner in which the people of that society relate to one another. Considering the way in which a society lives includes such areas as how the people make their living; where they live geographically; how they worship, recreate, make clothing, farm and cook. The **manner** in which the members of the society relate to one another would involve consideration of areas such as family customs, economic practices, civil laws, legal procedures, military tactics; as well as various types of social groupings (e.g., in Genesis 29:26 we find that Jacob would not have been deceived had he been familiar with the marriage customs in the land of Nahor; it is impossible to interpret properly I Peter 5:4 without an understanding of how the "chief shepherd" functioned in that day).

The way in which a people live within their environment molds their way of thinking. Therefore to understand the way in which a people think it is necessary to become acquainted with the way they live, bridging the cultural gap.

C.   **The Geographical Gap**

1.   **Problem** The geographical context of the Biblical writers is foreign to the modern day reader.

2.   **Solution**: This geographical gap may be bridged by a study of the geographical setting in which the events and writing of the Bible occurred. The problem is accentuated, however, by the fact that the writers themselves lived in different geographical contexts (e.g., Paul in Rome, Daniel in Babylon, and Moses in the wilderness). The problem is further complicated by the fact that some places mentioned in ancient writings either no longer exist or are no longer called by the same name. The answers to these problems can only be found by using the spade of archaeology. This involves study in three general areas:

a.   **Political Geography**: In order to become acquainted with the cities, states and nations mentioned by the Biblical authors, we are dependent upon the research of the archaeologist. We are not necessarily looking to the archaeologist to substantiate the existence of a city or state, rather we are seeking facts concerning that place which will aid us in interpretation (e.g., it would be impossible to understand Elijah's run from Carmel to Jezreel in I Kings 18:42-46 without knowing the location of each and the distance between the two; archaeological evidence has greatly helped in understanding Isaiah 44:27-45:2 relative to the fall of Babylon).

b.   **Geological Geography**: In order to understand references to climate, land formations, seas and rivers, we depend in part on archaeological evidences and in part on maps, written descriptions, photography and modern travel. A problem in this area is that, though the physical features of the Middle East have not changed drastically since Bible days, in some instances the names for them have (e.g., Psalms 125:2 and Isaiah 2:2 will be much more appreciated when the topography of the area around Jerusalem is considered; the significance of II Kings 5:10, 12 will be better understood by a consideration of the rivers mentioned).

c.   **Botanical and Zoological Geography**: To understand allusions to plant life and animal life by Bible authors, we are dependent on both archaeology and plants and animals, and to study their characteristics and behavioral patterns (e.g., one cannot effectively interpret Proverbs 30:19-31, or Luke 13:32 without an understanding of the nature, habits and instincts of the creatures mentioned there; a study of Biblical botany will unfold the beauty of Song of Solomon 2:1-3).

Thus research into the political, geographical, botanical and zoological divisions of geography enable the interpreter to bridge the geographical gap.

D.   **The Historical Gap**

1.   **Problem**: The historical context of the Biblical writers differs greatly from that of the modern day reader.

2.   **Solution**: The way to bridge this historical gap is to become familiar with the historical setting for the events of the Bible and in which the writers lived. But this pursuit is complicated by the fact that the writers lived during a period spanning sixteen centuries, from Moses to John, and in a constantly changing world situation. In each era of history the world situation must be considered from three viewpoints.

a.   **Political Background**: In order to understand the significance of events and viewpoints in Scripture, the political background must be taken into account. Succeeding governments have differing effects upon the peoples under their control so that the total lives of individuals are definitely influenced by the political order of which they are a part, whether willingly or unwillingly. In order to interpret the actions of Bible characters and writers, one must do everything possible to place himself mentally within that political environment (e.g., the significance of Hosea 12:1 can only be comprehended in the light of the political relationships between Ephraim, Assyria and Egypt; we cannot understand why the disciples of Jesus misunderstood His statements in Matthew 20:21 and Acts 1:6 without recognizing the political concerns of the day).

b.   **Economic Background**: Another factor which must be taken into consideration in order to understand the significance of events and viewpoints in Scripture is the economic background of the period. The economic situation, whether local or universal, exerts great influence on a people's way of life. This is seen by the diversity or uniformity of occupations within a society and the resultant creation of rich and poor classes. The interpreter must imagine himself in the economic situation of the passage he is interpreting (e.g., the economic wealth and need in the Early Church played a major role in fusing the Jewish and Gentile believers; see Acts 11:27-30).

c.   **Religious Background**: Finally, in order to understand properly events and viewpoints in Scripture, the religious background must also be considered. Societies have always been greatly influenced by religion; the lives of individuals often revolve around, or are at least affected by their religions. Throughout Scripture God's people are seen in relation to other religious groups as either being influenced by them or in conflict with them. Hence the need for the interpreter to place himself within the religious frame of reference of the writers and characters of Scripture (e.g., the significance of Leviticus 18:9-14 cannot be estimated apart from an evaluation of the Canaanite religions; Paul's conflict in Ephesus can only be brought to life by research into the religious context of Diana worship in Ephesus; Acts 19:24-41).

Thus a study into the political economic and religious background aids the interpreter in bridging the historical gap.

IN SUMMARY

Therefore, realizing the importance of the Bible in the Christian life, it becomes essential that we understand how to use the Bible. Most Christians have understood that they should read, meditate on, memorize, and live the Bible, but now a rapidly increasing number are realizing that to facilitate all these better they must also study the Bible.

The Bible is a book that is at times easy and at other times difficult to understand. Anyone who has read very far in its pages has soon discovered that he must interpret to discern its meaning. This is true not only because the Bible is Deity speaking to humanity but also because God used human vessels through which to communicate His truth. In many ways He adapted and communicated His message through their own frames of reference. As noted, this immediately presents four major problems to the Bible student:

1.   The Bible was written in three languages that are no longer in use today.

2.   The culture contexts of the Bible writers are very different from that of today.

3.   The geographical context of the Bible writers is foreign to most students today.

4.   The historical context of the Bible writers differs greatly from that of today.

These four foundational problems in understanding Scripture are like gaps that exist between the Bible writer's and the Bible student's frames of reference. These understanding gaps must be bridged as illustrated below:

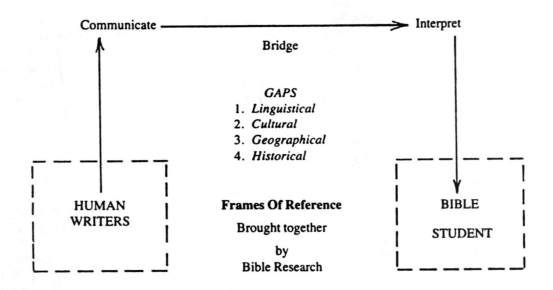

In order to build this bridge between our understanding and theirs, certain tools are needed. You will become familiar with a few of these through this course; others are listed on the following pages. You will also become familiar with several methods of using these tools at which point it should become evident that Bible research is a most worthwhile endeavor.

VI.   SUGGESTED RESEARCH TOOLS

As in any building, all tradesmen need certain **tools** to help them accomplish the task, so it is with the Bible. All students need tools to help. The task is communication of Divine truth; the tools needed to bridge the communication gap between ourselves and the writers as well as to our own generation. Each of the following are only partial listings of these tools for gap-bridging.

THE LINGUISTIC GAP

Concordances

New Englishman's Greek Concordance (Zondervan).
New Englishman's Hebrew & Chaldee Concordance(Zondervan).
Greek-English Concordance to the New Testament, J.B. Smith (Herald Press).
Strong's Exhaustive Concordance (Abingdon).
Young's Analytical Concordance (Eerdman's).

Lexicons

Analytical Greek Lexicon (Zondervan).
Analytical Hebrew & Chaldee Lexicon, B. Davidson (MacDonald).
Greek-English Lexicon, Arndt & Gingrich (University of Chicago Press).
Greek-English Lexicon, T.S. Green (Zondervan).
Hebrew-English Lexicon, W. Gesenius (Oxford).
New Thayer's Greek-English Lexicon (Zondervan).

Lexical Aids

Dictionary of Old Testament Words, Aaron Pick (Kregel).
Expositor's Greek Testament, W. Robertson Nicoll (Eerdman's).
Expository Dictionary of New Testament Words, W.E. Vine (Revell).
Grammatical Insights into the New Testament, N. Turner (T.& T. Clark).
Lexical Aids for Students of New Testament Greek, B. Metzger (Theological Book Agency, Dist.).
New Testament Words, William Barclay (SCM Press).
New Testament Word Studies, J.A. Bengel (Kregel).
Synonyms of the New Testament, R.B. Girdleston. (Eerdman's).
Syntax of the Moods and Tenses, E. Burton (T.&T. Clark).
Theological Dictionary of the New Testament, Kittel (Ed. Eerdman's).
Word Pictures in the New Testament, A.T. Robertson (Broadman Press).
Word Studies in the New Testament, M.R. Vincent (Eerdman's).

Grammars

Essentials of New Testament Greek, J.H. Huddilston (MacMillan).
Grammar of the Greek New Testament, A.T. Robertson (Broadman Press).
Greek Grammar of the New Testament, Blass & Debruner (University of Chicago Press).

Hebrew Grammar, Wm. Gesenius (Oxford University).
Introductory Hebrew Grammar, R.L. Harris (Eerdman's).
Manual Grammar of the Greek New Testament, Dana & Mantey (Macmillan).
New Testament Greek for Beginners, J.G. Machen.
Practical Grammar for Classical Hebrew, J.Weingren (Oxford).
Figures of Speech Used in the Bible, E.W. Bullinger (Baker).

THE CULTURAL GAP

All the Holy Days and Holidays of the Bible, H. Lockyer (Zondervan).
All the Trades and Occupations of the Bible, H. Lockyer (Zondervan).
Archaeology and Ancient Testament, J.L. Kelso (Zondervan).
The Bible and Archaeology, J.A. Thompson (Eerdman's).
Biblical Archaeology, G.E. Wright (Westminster Press).
Everyday Life in Bible Times, (National Geographic Society).
Insights into Bible Times and Customs, Weiss (Moody).
The Land the Book, W.M. Thompson (Harper & Brothers).
Life and Times of Jesus the Messiah, A. Edersheim (Eerdman's).
Manners and Customs of the Bible, J. Freeman (Logos International).
Manners and Customs of Bible Lands, F.H. Wright (Moody).
Orientations in Bible Lands, E.W. Rice (American Sunday School Union).

Bible Dictionaries

Bible Dictionary, Smith (Holt, Rinehart & Winston).
David Dictionary of the Bible (Revell).
International Standard Bible Encyclopedia (Eerdman's).
The New Bible Dictionary (Eerdman's).
Pictorial Bible Dictionary, M.C. Tenney (Zondervan).
Ungers Bible Dictionary (Moody).

THE GEOGRAPHICAL GAP

All the Animals of the Bible Lands, G. Cunsdale (Zondervan).
Animals and Birds of the Bible, B.L. Goddard (A.P. & A.).
Baker's Bible Atlas, Pfeiffer (Baker).
Geography of the Bible, D. Baly (Harper & Brothers).
The Macmillan Bible Atlas (Macmillan).
Oxford Bible Atlas (Oxford Press).
The Wycliffe Historical Geography of Bible Lands, Pfeiffer & Vos. (Moody).

See also "Bible Dictionaries" listed under Cultural Tools.

THE HISTORICAL GAP

Archaeology & Bible History, J.P. Free (Van Kampen Press).
Archaeology and the Old Testament, Under (Zondervan).
The Bible and Archaeology, J.A. Thompson (Paternoster Press).
Bible History - Old Testament, A. Edersheim (Eerdman's).
Old Testament Bible History, Edersheim (Eerdman's).

The Life and Times of Jesus the Messiah, A. Edersheim (Eerdman's).
The Works of Flavius Josephus (Kregel).

See also "Bible Dictionaries" listed under Cultural Tools.

CHAPTER THREE

METHODS AND PRINCIPLES OF RESEARCH

It has been said:

> "Methods are many, Principles few,
> Methods may vary, Principles never do."

I. METHODS OF BIBLE RESEARCH

A. Definition of "Method" (as used here)

A suitable and convenient arrangement of things, proceedings or ideas; the natural or regular disposition of separate things or parts; convenient order for transacting business, or for comprehending any complicated subject.
(Noah Webster's Dictionary)

A way; system; course; course of procedure; classification; logical arrangement; orderly.
(Collin's Graphic Dictionary)

Thus when we speak of a "method" of Bible study, Bible research, we mean a suitable and convenient order, procedure and logical arrangement of Bible subjects.

B. Seven Methods of Study

Seven major methods of Bible research are presented in this course with their respective assignments.

1. WORD Studies

2. CHARACTER Studies

3. PLACE Studies

4. TEXTUAL Studies

5. TOPICAL Thematic Studies

6. PASSAGE Studies

7. BOOK Studies

II. PRINCIPLES OF BIBLE RESEARCH

A. Definition of "Principle" (as used here)

A general truth; a law comprehending many subordinate truths; such as the **principles** of morality, of law, of government, etc.
(Noah Webster's Dictionary)

A source or origin; that from which anything proceeds; a fundamental truth or tenet; an elementary proposition; a settled rule of action.
(Collins Graphic Dictionary)

Thus when we speak of a "principle" of Bible Research, we mean a general truth, or fundamental truth, a settled rule of action.

B.   **Six Principles of Bible Research**

Following are six major principles in Bible Research, each of which form successive links in a chain in proper research.

1.   **OBSERVATION** – What does the Bible say on that subject? Observation is the collection or gathering of all the data in Scripture on any particular subject.

2.   **INTERPRETATION** - What does the Bible mean?

What does it mean to me? What did it mean to them?
Myles Coverdale, AD1535 says: "It shall greatly help ye to understand Scripture, If thou mark not only what is spoken or written, But of whom, and to whom, with what words, at what time, where, to what intent, with what circumstances, Considering what goeth before and what followeth." To interpret Scripture then we must therefore investigate:

a.   WHAT - What is actually being said (not "reading between the lines").

b.   OF WHOM - Who is being talked bout (Acts 8:34. "Of whom speaketh the prophet?).

c.   TO WHOM - Who is being spoken to?

d.   WITH WHAT WORDS - In what language (consider why such terms are used)?

e.   AT WHAT TIME - When was it written (e.g., James written before Romans)?

f.   WHERE - The writer's circumstances and perspective (e.g., Paul in jail when he writes Philippians).

g.   TO WHAT INTENT - The writer's purpose in writing (e.g., Galatians Epistle).

h.   WITH WHAT CIRCUMSTANCES - What circumstances were the recipients in (e.g., I Peter, "Sufferings")?

i.   WHAT GOETH BEFORE - The preceding context, what flows into the verse.

j.   WHAT FOLLOWETH - The succeeding context, what flows out of the verse.

All of this belongs to the field of Interpretation or Hermeneutics.

3.   **ORGANIZATION** - What do I do with it?

Now that one has all this information, and interpretation, what do I do with it? How do I organize it?

A heap of stones does not make a building anymore than a quantity of Scriptures make a message!

It is not enough just to quote fifty references from Strong's Concordance! There are many ways to organize a subject, but it is generally good to use the building method of line upon line, in logical, sequential manner, thus building a message into the hearers.

Generally speaking, organization belongs to Homiletics. Organization will basically follow:

    a.   Introduction, statement of proposition, what you hope to communicate to hearers.

    b.   Main Body of Message - The material, illustrations, etc.

    c.   Conclusion - The practical application of all that has gone before.

4.   **PRESENTATION** - How do I communicate it?

This also belongs to the field of Homiletics. Presentation has to do with manner or method of communicating the message, whether preaching or teaching the Word.

5.   **APPLICATION** - How can I apply it practically?

Information without application is incomplete. How can people apply truth to their lives in a practical manner?

If we have numbers 1-4 without this then the message has failed in its total purpose.

Application is making the meaning relevant.

Knowledge - the possession of facts.

Understanding - the interpretation of facts.

Wisdom - the application of facts.

People need not only to know the rules of the game of life but how they apply to them.

The principle of application is seen in the following triangle:

Principle of Application

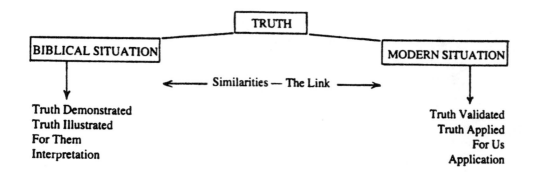

25

Theologically speaking then, "application" is the taking of truth communicated (revealed and directed) to one person or group of people and making it relate to another person or group of people. The basis for this is the understanding that God's principles of truth are timeless - **TRUTH IS TRUTH** in every generation.

6.   **EVALUATION** - What did the people learn? How and what was communicated?

All need to evaluate the communication of the Word. How much is taught can really be evaluated by how much is learned.

The ultimate aim of Bible Research is to be the best communicator of Scripture and its life-changing and life-giving principles to the people to whom we minister!

Section II
TOOLS FOR RESEARCH

CHAPTER FOUR

STRONG'S EXHAUSTIVE CONCORDANCE
By James Strong

INTRODUCTORY

The following explanation concerning the use of the Strong's Concordance is based upon the older Copyrighted Edition (1890), by Abingdon Press, New York.

However, a newer edition, printed by Thomas Nelson Publishers, New York (1984) improves upon the original volume in several significant ways, as noted here.

> Modern easy-to-read typesetting
> Most accurate numbering system
> Corrections of errors in previous editions
> Improved design and format
> Variant spellings of proper names from modern versions of the Bible, with definitions and pronunciations
> Appendix to Main Concordance reset and corrections made
> A key Verse Comparison Chart of six major translations of the Scriptures is provided. i.e., KJV, NKJV, NASB, NIV, RSV and TEV
> The Laws of the Bible
> Teachings and Illustrations of Christ
> Jewish Calendar and Jewish Feasts
> Monies, Weights and Measures Chart

This edition is strongly recommended to the student for use. However, the following is based upon the older editions, but the same procedure is applicable for the new editions of Strong's Concordance also.

I.   THE PURPOSE OF THE BOOK (Its Value and Use)

The purpose of this book is to list every occurrence of every word used in the King James' Version of the Bible and link each word with its specific Hebrew or Greek counterpart. This is done without necessitating any knowledge of the original languages on the part of the student. Its value is derived mainly from its accomplishment of its exhaustive purpose.

This book can be used in three main areas:

A.   It can be used for finding the reference to a partially known verse of Scripture. If the student can only remember one significant word in a verse, by using this book he can locate its reference.

B.   It can be used for finding the Hebrew or Greek word, and its definition, behind any English word in the King James Version of the Bible. Without knowing Hebrew or Greek the student can look up the original words involved in any particular text he is studying, and find their derivation and basic definition.

C.   It can be used for doing "word studies" in Scripture. This could include studying the significance and usage of a single word throughout Scripture, comparing words in Scripture (e.g. synonyms or antonyms), or studying a subject relative to one single word.

II   A DESCRIPTION OF THE BOOK (Its Design and Parts)

The Strong's Concordance consists of the following parts:

A.   Introductory Page - This page includes a general preface to the book setting forth its purpose, explaining its design and giving directions for its use. This page should be red carefully, especially noting the key to the abbreviation of the names of the books of the Bible. (Song of Solomon is called Canticles and is abbreviated "Ca".)

B.   Main Concordance

   1.   Listings

   This comprises the major portion of the book, covering 1,211 pages. Here every word (with the exception of those mentioned on the Introductory Page) that is used in the Authorized King James Version of the Bible is listed in alphabetical order. Under each word is a complete listing of every Scripture reference in which the particular word occurs along with a written out portion of that verse. In each written out phrase the word under consideration is abbreviated by its initial letter which is also italicized and followed by an inverted period.

   abide

   Ge 19:2 we will a· in the street all night

   2.   Page Headings

   Each page is divided into three columns which are meant to be followed from left to right. At the top of each page on its outside corner will be found not only the page number but also two words, one above another. The top word is that word which is the first to begin its heading on the left-hand page of each **double** page. The exception to this occurs when a word begun on a previous page continues its listing through the left-hand page and into the right-hand page. Then the word begun on a previous page is listed on top on both pages of a double page (see pages 61-62). The bottom word indicates the last word on the right-hand page to begin its listing. If there is only one word at the top of a double page, this indicates that both pages are filled with its listing; that it has its beginning on a preceding page and its ending on a succeeding page.

   3.   Dictionary Numbers

   At the right-hand side of each column is a number or an inverted quotation mark (a ditto "). The ditto automatically refers back to the nearest previously mentioned number. (Note - The New Strong's Concordance lists the number and not the ditto).

   The regular print numbers beside the Old Testament references are meant to lead the student to the Hebrew or Chaldee word used in that verse. The numbers correspond with the numbers beside each word in the Hebrew-Chaldee dictionary at the back of the Concordance. The student should be careful not to confuse these two distinct numbering systems.

abounding

Pro	8:24	no fountains a· with water	3513
1 Co	15:58	always a· in the work of the Lord	4052
Col	2:7	a· therein with thanksgiving	"

The numbers in the main concordance may be preceded by an asterisk (*) indicating a difference in translation in the Revised Standard Version. The obelist (†) and the double obelist (‡) mark similar changes.

4.   **Addenda**

This is an addition to the main concordance including additions and corrections to it. It covers pages 1211 to 1217. When a word appears in the addenda adding references that are not to be found in the main concordance then a caret mark (^) appears immediately after the word in that **main** concordance. If an entire word has been left out of the main concordance then a horizontal caret mark (>) appears in its alphabetical place in the main concordance. Thus the student need only refer to the addenda when he finds these caret marks in the main concordance. In all other respects the addenda follows the same format as the main concordance.

5.   **Appendix**

The appendix contains a listing of all the references (book, chapter and verse only) in which the forty-seven particles not listed in the main concordance are used. These are listed in this manner primarily because of the frequency of their usage in Scripture. This section covers pages 1219 to 1340.

6.   **Comparative Concordance**

The older editions contain a Comparative Concordance with Preface, Explanation, of the Authorized (King James' Version) and Revised Versions of the Scriptures setting out the different word (or different words) in each version.

This section covers 262 pages including its Notanda (a small section dealing with extreme variations or alterations in the versions) and a short Addenda.

Its purpose is to bring together in a sharper focus the differences between the two translations, the Authorized and Revised Versions.

7.   **Hebrew and Chaldee Dictionary**

This section comprises in alphabetical listing according to the Hebrew alphabet of all the words used in the Bible. The student should take note of the introductory page to this section, its Preface and Plan of the Book and especially its explanation of the Abbreviations and Symbols used in the Dictionary.

Each word has **a number** immediately preceding its listing which corresponds to its English equivalents in the main concordance.

The Hebrew (or Greek) word comes immediately after the number.

The Hebrew word is followed by its **English transliteration in bold print.**

Next follows the **English pronunciation** in italics.

Then a concise **etymology and definition** of the word follows often using abbreviated words from the introduction to explain the word's signification.

Finally, after the colon and dash(: -) are given **all the different English words** that somewhere in the King James version are used to translate the thought of that particular Hebrew word.

CAUTION: The words that appear **after** the colon and dash (: -) are not a part of the definition of that word. This section is numbered from 1 to 126.

Note: Immediately following the Hebrew Dictionary is a page listing the place where the Hebrew and English Bibles differ in the division of the text into chapters and verses.

8. **Greek Dictionary**

The Greek Dictionary follows the same format as the Hebrew Dictionary, the only difference being that the numbers assigned to words are printed in italics to allow a distinction between the two languages in the main concordance. This section is numbered from 1 to 79.

Again, the student needs to read the Plan of the Book and especially the Abbreviations and Symbols employed.

Note: At the conclusion of the Greek Dictionary is a short list of variant verse numberings between the Greek and English New Testaments.

WORKSHOP EXAMPLES

Following is an example from both the Hebrew and Greek Dictionaries illustrating an eightfold approach in the use of Strong's Concordance for the discovery of the meaning of a word.

HEBREW/CHALDEE DICTIONARY

The Scripture in Isaiah 56:7 tells us that God's house is to be "a house of PRAYER for all nations."

To discover the meaning of the word *"prayer"* here, we would follow this procedure once the Dictionary number has been discovered from the right hand column in Strong's Concordance.

8605. תְּפִלָּה **tᵉphillâh,** *tef-il-law';* from 6419; *intercession, supplication;* by impl. a *hymn:*—prayer.

6419. פָּלַל **ipâlal,** *paw-lal';* a prim. root; to *judge* (officially or mentally); by extens. to *intercede, pray:*—intreat, judge (-ment), (make) pray (-er, -ing), make supplication.

1. **The English Word** - Prayer.

2. **The Strong's Concordance Number** - SC 8605

3. **The Hebrew** - (Not compulsory unless knowledgeable of such).

4. **The Transliteration** - tephillah.

5. **The Pronunciation** - tef-il-law

6. **The Etymology and Definition of the word** - From SC 6419; intercession, supplication; by implic. a hymn.

    (Note also SC 6419 as above and definition of word.)

7. **The Ways the word is translated** - Prayer.

8. **Summary of word definition** - The word "prayer" here speaks of intercession, supplication and can be a hymn of prayer, or a hymn of intercession and supplication to God in His house.

GREEK DICTIONARY

The Scripture tells us in Ephesians 4:1 that we are "to WALK worthy of the vocation wherewith we are called."

To discover the meaning of the word "*walk*" here, we would follow the same procedure as above once the Dictionary Number from Strong's has been discovered from the right hand column.

The number here is SC 4043 and now we turn to the Greek Dictionary to find the information recorded there.

4043. περιπατέω **pĕrĭpatĕō**, *per-ee-pat-eh'-o;* from *4012* and *3961;* to *tread all around,* i.e. *walk* at large (espec. as proof of ability); fig. to *live, deport oneself, follow* (as a companion or votary):—go, be occupied with, walk (about).

4012. περί **pĕrĭ**, *per-ee';* from the base of *4008;* prop. *through* (all over), i.e. *around;* fig. *with respect to;* used in various applications, of place, cause or time (with the gen. denoting the *subject* or *occasion* or *superlative* point; with the acc. the *locality, circuit, matter, circumstance* or general *period*):—(there-) about, above, against, at, on behalf of, X and

3961. πατέω **patĕō**, *pat-eh'-o;* from a der. prob. of *3817* (mean. a "path"); to *trample* (lit. or fig.):—tread (down, under foot).

1. **The English Word** - Walk.

2. **The Strong's Concordance Number** - SC 4043

3. **The Greek** - Not compulsory unless knowledgeable of Greek).

4. **The Transliteration** - peripateo.

5. **The Pronunciation** - per-ee-pat-eh'-o.

6. **The Etymology and Definition of the word** - From SC 4012 and 3961; to tread all around, i.e., walk at large (epec. as proof of ability); fig. to live, deport oneself, follow (as a companion or votary): -

   (Note:- To discover more fully the etymology and definition of the word, the student would need to refer to the other numbers, SC 4012 and 3961, as this word is made up of at lease two other Greek words as the above example from Strong's shows).

7. **The Ways the word is translated** - ":- go, be occupied with, walk (about)."

8. **Summary of word definition -**

   The word "*walk*" speaks of "the way one treads around, how he lives, deports himself, how he follows someone."

34

III. HOW TO USE THE BOOK

The way in which a student uses this book is of necessity dependent upon the purposes for which he desires to use it.

The basic procedure is that of finding the word that is being studied in the Main Concordance and using the number system to find its corresponding Hebrew or Greek word in the Dictionaries at the back of the book and then to discover its meaning by following the above example procedures.

STRONG'S WORKSHOP

assignment #1

TOOLS NEEDED: Strong's Concordance

ASSIGNMENT: Work through the following questions and statements. If you have any difficulty, raise your hand and an instructor will assist you.

1.   Foundational to the study of Scripture and the use of a Strong's Concordance is a knowledge of the names of the books of the Bible, their order, and their abbreviations. Can you recite the sixty-six books of the Bible in order? If not, learn them immediately. Reviewing them several times daily in the next few weeks will help to firmly implant them in your mind.

Write out the books that these abbreviations stand for:

La -   Ca -

Joe -   De -

Jg -   Mic -

II Th -   Ps -

Re -   Mr -

Le -   Ne -

Ob -   Jas -

Ga -

Write the abbreviations for these books:

Philemon -   I Corinthians -

Philippians -   II Chronicles -

Ezra -   Zephaniah -

Esther -   Zechariah -

Joshua -   Matthew -

2. Since the words considered in Strong's are listed alphabetically, the student should not have any difficulty finding the word he wants to look up. Just to be sure, write the page numbers on which the following words occur:

Angel   -

Triumph   -

Lamp   -

Faith   -

Swine   -

STRONG'S WORKSHOP

assignment #2

TOOLS NEEDED: Strong's Concordance and a King James Version of the Bible.

ASSIGNMENT: Work through the following directions. If you have any difficulty, raise your hand and an instructor will assist you.

Have you ever known a verse of Scripture but couldn't find where it was? With a Strong's Concordance you can solve that problem. If you know at least one significant word in the verse you can find its location by using your Strong's. The following are phrases from the Bible. Use your Strong's to find the book, chapter, and verse in which they are found. To make this as quick and easy as possible, circle the word that you think is used least often in the Bible and look it up to find your verse. Then use your Bible to check your answer.

EXAMPLE:

II Timothy 2:13 "If we believe not, yet he **abideth** faithful".

1. "Their Redeemer is strong"

2. "as a shepherd divideth his sheep from the goats"

3. "and the stars of heaven fell unto the earth."

4. "remove thy foot from evil"

5. "sanctify yourselves: for tomorrow the Lord will do wonders among you"

6. "we ought to obey God rather than men"

7. "order my steps in Thy word"

8. "God is come to prove you"

9. "whose God is their belly"

STRONG'S WORKSHOP

assignment #3

TOOLS NEEDED: Strong's Concordance.

ASSIGNMENT: Work through the following directions. If you have any difficulty, raise your hand and an instructor will assist you.

By using your Strong's Concordance write down how many different Hebrew and Greek words are translated in the King James Version by the English words below. First, look up the English word and then list the dictionary numbers as illustrated below.

EXAMPLE:

abide:

	Hebrew - 12		*Greek* - 4
	3885	1481	3306
	3427	7937	1961
	2583	3867	3887
	935	3557	4357
	5975	2342	
	1692	6965	

restore: *Hebrew* -   *Greek* -

preach: *Hebrew* -   *Greek* -

doctrine: *Hebrew* -   *Greek* -

praise: *Hebrew* -   *Greek* -

Incense: *Hebrew* -   *Greek* -

STRONG'S WORKSHOP

assignment #4

TOOLS NEEDED: Strong's Concordance and a King James Version Bible.

ASSIGNMENT: Work through the following directions. If you have any difficulty, raise your hand and an instructor will assist you.

Look up the words indicated and supply the following information about each one. (Be sure to write out any abbreviated words.) Follow the eightfold procedure as in the examples.

1. The English word

2. The Strong's Concordance Dictionary Number

3. The Hebrew or Greek word (not compulsory if languages of same not known)

4. The Transliteration of the Hebrew or Greek word

5. The Pronunciation

6. The Etymology and Definition of the word

7. The Ways in which the word is translated in the King James Version

8. Summary in brief of word definition, or, what your research tells you about that word.

WORDS TO BE WORKED THROUGH FROM BOTH OLD AND NEW TESTAMENTS

Rejoice – Philippians 4:4

1. The English word -

2. The Strong's Concordance Number -

3. The Greek -

4. The Transliteration -

5. The Pronunciation -

6. The Etymology and Definition of the word -

7. The Ways the word is translated -

8. Summary of word definition -

Rejoice – Philippians 3:3

1.   The English word -

2.   The Strong's Concordance Number -

3.   The Greek -

4.   The Transliteration -

5.   The Pronunciation -

6.   The Etymology and Definition of the word -

7.   The Ways the word is translated -

8.   Summary of word definition -

Perish – Proverbs 29:18

1.   The English word -

2.   The Strong's Concordance Number -

3.   The Hebrew -

4.   The Transliteration -

5.   The Pronunciation -

6.   The Etymology and Definition of the word -

7.   The Ways the word is translated -

8.   Summary of word definition -

Slew – I John 3:12

1.   The English word -

2.   The Strong's Concordance Number -

3.   The Greek -

4.   The Transliteration -

5.   The Pronunciation -

6.   The Etymology and Definition of the word -

7.   The Ways the word is translated -

8.   Summary of word definition -

Thanksgiving – Psalm 100:4

1.   The English word -

2.   The Strong's Concordance Number -

3.   The Hebrew -

4.   The Transliteration -

5.   The Pronunciation -

6.   The Etymology and Definition of the word -

7.   The Ways the word is translated -

8.   Summary of word definition -

CHAPTER FIVE

THE NEW ENGLISHMAN'S CONCORDANCES
– GREEK CONCORDANCE –

I.   THE PURPOSE OF THE BOOK

The purpose of this book is to list every occurrence of every Greek word in the Greek New Testament and to show how it was translated in the King James Version of the New Testament. Its value is derived not only from its exhaustiveness, but also from the fact that it allows the student to "get behind" the English translation and study how certain Greek words are used throughout the New Testament. It enables the student to do a "proper" word study. It helps him discover what God meant by a particular word that He used in the New Testament. Undoubtedly the element that makes this concordance outstanding in its field is that by utilizing the numbering system of Strong's Concordance, it enables a person who has no knowledge of Greek to conveniently locate every usage of any Greek word in the New Testament.

II.   A DESCRIPTION OF THE BOOK

Introduction

The first few pages of this book contain introduction giving its history, describing its value, and explaining its design.

A.   The Concordance

This comprises the main portion of the book, covering 872 pages. Here every Greek word (excluding proper names which are found on pages 818-872) that is used in the Greek New Testament is listed in alphabetical order (according to the Greek alphabet). Each Greek word is first written in Greek and then an English transliteration is placed next to it in italics. Under each word is a complete listing of every New Testament reference in which that particular word occurs along with a written out portion of that verse. In each written out phrase the King James Version English translation of the Greek word under consideration is printed in italics. Each page is divided into two columns which are meant to be followed from left to right.

To the left of and slightly higher than each Greek word is a number. This number corresponds to the number given that same Greek word in Strong's Exhaustive Concordance. This is what enables a non-Greek student to utilize this concordance effectively. The numbers to the right of the Greek word indicate its root word(s).

The letters "rt" show that the word has the same root as the word whose number is given (example, page 429, #2875).

The letters "cf" (i.e., page 429, #2875) refer to a related word such as a synonym.

The numbers in brackets (i.e., page 827, #1446) signify words from the Hebrew and Chaldee Dictionary of Strong's Concordance. Occasionally small numbers or letters are used within a listing to indicate certain things. The explanation of these is to be found at the beginning of the listing of that word.

The letters "e.g." (where used) denote that the number given designates a word that is simply another form of the word under consideration.

B.   English–Greek Index

This is an alphabetical listing of all the English words in the New Testament of the King James Version. Under each word is given the one or more Greek words that are translated by the English word. The page number where that Greek word can be found in the concordance is then given to the right of it. A dash in the right hand column indicates that the word is to be found on the same page as the word preceding it. This section covers pages 873 to 943.

C.   Greek–English Index

This is an alphabetical listing of all the Greek words in the Greek New Testament. Under each word is given the one or more English words that are used to translate each Greek word. The page number where each Greek word can be found in the concordance is then given to the right of it. This section covers pages 945 to 1020.

D.   Appendix

This contains two parts in which added listings and special classifications are to a few pronouns, articles and conjunctions. This section is numbered from 1 to 14.

III.   HOW TO USE THE BOOK

For the student without knowledge of Greek the use of this book will be most effective when using it in connection with Strong's Concordance (and possibly the New Thayer's Lexicon). When a student desires to study a word in the New Testament, he should first go to Strong's Concordance and find the number of its Greek equivalent. Then he can look up that word in this concordance to study its use in the New Testament.

Workshop Example

From the Introduction to this Greek Concordance we adapt the following (The New Englishman's Greek Concordance, Copyright, by Associated Publishers and Authors, Inc. 1972 edition).

The English word "love" is translated from four Greek words as noted on the Diagram from the Concordance. There is no English word that is the exact equivalent of any Greek word. It is not necessarily because the translation is faulty.

If the student *only* used Strong's, then he will need to be switching back and forth over a number of words once he finds out how the Greek word is translated in the King James Version, as well as its root word (or words) and how they may be translated.

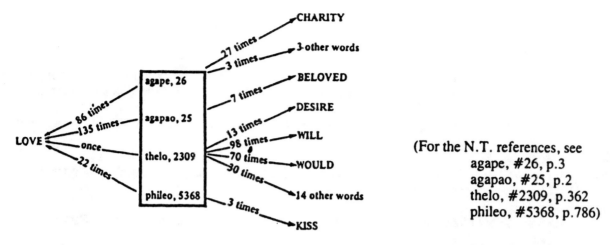

(For the N.T. references, see
    agape, #26, p.3
    agapao, #25, p.2
    thelo, #2309, p.362
    phileo, #5368, p.786)

We quote the following. "In the middle figures above we have indicated four of the Greek words which are sometimes translated "love". On the right you see the reference to 23 English words, which are sometimes employed to translate one or the other of these four Greek words."

One can see what work and time would be involved in the use of Strong's *only* to discover all the ways and words used to translate the Greek words for "love".

However, the New Englishman's Greek Concordance does it for you as the New Testament references for "love" (from Greek words) show.
Refer to #25, #26, #27, #2309 and #5368.

NOTE:

A.   The student is also referred to The Word Study Concordance (Tyndale House Publishers, Inc., Wheaton, Illinois, 1972, 1978), which fulfills the same purpose (with additions) as the New Englishman's Greek Concordance.

      This is a two volume set which includes the New Testament and the Word Study Concordance geared to Strong's, Arndt/Gingrich Lexicon, Moulton & Gedon Greek Concordance, and Kittel's Theological Dictionary of the Old Testament.

B.   The New Englishman's Greek Concordance published by Hendrickson Publishers, Massachusetts fulfills the same role as the earlier editions of this work by other Publishers. However, it does have several other helpful additions to it, as noted in the following.

    1.   The New Englishman's Greek Concordance (Wigram-Green, 1982) has been expanded by the addition of a *lexicon*, making it both a *concordance* and a *lexicon*.

    2.   References have been added for the Bible student to turn to these additional sources for discussion of any word under study. These works are referenced:

        Strong's Exhaustive Concordance (numbering system)
        Arndt-Gingrich Greek English Lexicon of the New Testament (page   number)
        Kittel's Theological Dictionary of the New Testament (volume, page number)
        Thayer's Greek-English Lexicon to the New Testament (page, column number).

3. Proper Names have been placed in the main concordance in alphabetical order instead of having to refer to another section, as in previous and other editions.

4. The Index-English and Greek has been eliminated as the Strong's numbering system is already there.

5. The Greek-English Index has also been eliminated as this information is at the head of each word.

Other points of interest are in the Introduction to the New Englishman's Greek Concordance and Lexicon.
However the use of this "tool" is the same as other editions.

NEW ENGLISHMAN'S

GREEK WORKSHOP

TOOLS NEEDED: New Englishman's Greek Concordance and Strong's Workshop Assignment #4.

ASSIGNMENT: Work through the following directions. If you have any difficulty, raise your hand and an instructor will assist you.

The full benefit of the Greek Concordance will not be recognized until the student learns how to utilize it in connection with "word studies" later on in the semester. The following workshop will serve primarily to familiarize the student with the Concordance. It is based upon Strong's Workshop Assignment #4 and the student should refer to it for the basic information needed below. Then look up the following words in your Greek Concordance and list all the Scripture references for each way the Greek word is translated in the King James Version.

EXAMPLE:
1.   **SLEW – I John 3:12**

   A.   Strong's Number - SC 4969
   B.   Ways word is translated -
   Kill - Rev. 6:4
   slay/slain - I Jn 3:12; Rev. 5:6, 9, 12; 6:9; 13:8; 18:24
   wounded - Rev. 13:3

2.   **REJOICE – Philippians 4:4**

   A.   Strong's Number -
   B.   Ways word is translated -

   *

   *

   *

   *

3.   **REJOICE – Philippians 3:3**

   A.   Strong's Number -
   B.   Ways word is translated -

   *

   *

   *

   *

THE NEW ENGLISHMAN'S CONCORDANCES
– HEBREW CONCORDANCE –

I.   THE PURPOSE OF THE BOOK

This book is a companion to the Englishman's Greek Concordance. It is an essential tool if one wishes to study words or topics right through Scripture.

The purpose of this book is to list every occurrence of every Hebrew or Chaldee (now better known as Aramaic) word in the Old Testament and show how it is translated in the King James Version of the Old Testament.

Its value is derived not only from its exhaustiveness but also from the fact that it allows the student to "get behind" the English translation and study how certain Hebrew words are used throughout the Old Testament. It enables him to discover what God meant by a particular word that He used in the Old Testament.

It is also keyed to Strong's numbering system so that it enables one who has no knowledge of Hebrew to conveniently locate every use of any Hebrew/Chaldee word in the Old Testament.

II.   A DESCRIPTION OF THE BOOK

A.   Introduction

The first few pages of this book contain a general introduction giving its history, describing its value and explaining its design (pp. vii-xxx). This is essential reading to make the best use of the book. The example given on page ix of the word WALK illustrates the value of this concordance. This is seen in the following workshop example taken from the text.

WORKSHOP EXAMPLE

From the introduction to this Hebrew concordance we adapt the following.

The English word *"walk"* is translated from eight Hebrew words as noted on the Diagram from the concordance. There is no English word that is the exact equivalent of any Hebrew word. It is not necessarily because the translation is faulty.

If the student only used Strong's, then he will need to be switching back and forth over a number of words once he finds out how the Hebrew word is translated in the King James, as well as its root word (or words) and how they may be translated.

B.   The Concordance

This comprises the main portion of the book, covering 1360 pages, listing every Hebrew word in the Old Testament in Hebrew alphabetical order.

The Strong's number appears to the left and above the Hebrew word. Where a number appears on the right corner of the column opposite the Strong's number, it indicates either root words, and/or related words, synonyms or antonyms which may be used to compare the word under study for clearer understanding.

The Hebrew word is first written, with a pronunciation guide - not a direct transliteration - to the right of it. After this may be Ch., where words come from Ezra or Daniel. This means Chaldee or Aramaic, as it is usually called today. There may be other helpful grammatical abbreviations also, indicating the part of the speech of the word. Underneath are listed all the Old Testament references to that Hebrew word, with a brief quote from the verse in which it appears, the Hebrew word under consideration being printed in italics. Verbs are listed in Biblical order under each conjunction and tense of the verb.

Note: Hebrew proper names are to be found on pages 1-78 of the Appendix.

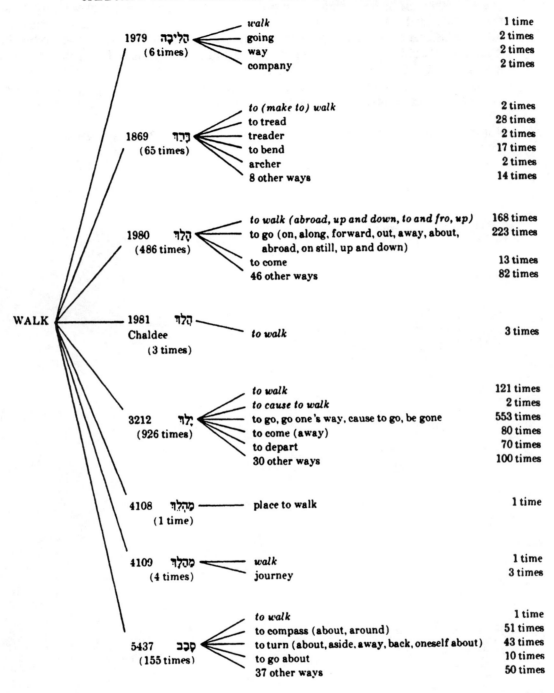

WALK

1979 הֲלִיכָה (6 times)
- *walk* — 1 time
- going — 2 times
- way — 2 times
- company — 2 times

1869 דָּרַךְ (65 times)
- *to (make to) walk* — 2 times
- to tread — 28 times
- treader — 2 times
- to bend — 17 times
- archer — 2 times
- 8 other ways — 14 times

1980 הָלַךְ (486 times)
- *to walk (abroad, up and down, to and fro, up)* — 168 times
- to go (on, along, forward, out, away, about, abroad, on still, up and down) — 223 times
- to come — 13 times
- 46 other ways — 82 times

1981 הֲלַךְ Chaldee (3 times)
- *to walk* — 3 times

3212 יָלַךְ (926 times)
- *to walk* — 121 times
- *to cause to walk* — 2 times
- to go, go one's way, cause to go, be gone — 553 times
- to come (away) — 80 times
- to depart — 70 times
- 30 other ways — 100 times

4108 מַהֲלָךְ (1 time)
- place to walk — 1 time

4109 מַהֲלָךְ (4 times)
- *walk* — 1 time
- journey — 3 times

5437 סָבַב (155 times)
- *to walk* — 1 time
- to compass (about, around) — 51 times
- to turn (about, aside, away, back, oneself about) — 43 times
- to go about — 10 times
- 37 other ways — 50 times

C. **Hebrew–English Index**

This is a listing of all Hebrew words in the Old Testament in alphabetical order, with the page number in the concordance on which appears opposite the word. Underneath each word are listed all the translations of it in the King James Version of the Bible. This section covers pages 1361 to 1458.

D. **English–Hebrew Index**

This is a listing in alphabetical order of all the English words in the Hebrew Old Testament and underneath each Hebrew word so translated, the page number on which appears in the concordance. This section covers pages 1459 to 1682.

E. **The Appendix**

This contains two sections: -

1. Hebrew and Chaldee Proper Names in the Strong's numbering order, and the Scripture reference/s for each (pp. 1-78).
   If number is missing in the main concordance, it is to be found here.

2. Table of Chapter and Verses in the English and Hebrew Bibles. First the English chapter and verses are given, followed by the Hebrew in parentheses. (cf. p. xiv para. 3). Eg., Psa 34:12 (13), 12 = King James Version versing. (13) = Hebrew versing.

III. **HOW TO USE THE BOOK**

For the student without the knowledge of Hebrew, the use of this book will be most effective when using it in connection with Strong's Concordance.

The same method for the Englishman's Greek Concordance is used for the Hebrew Concordance.

First, go to Strong's, find the word, the number, and look up the Hebrew Dictionary at the back for etymology, definition, etc. Then look up the same number in the Hebrew Concordance to find all its occurrences in the Old Testament.

When studying a verb, e.g., *walk*, S.C. 1980, the listing is arranged according to CONJUNCTION and TENSE.

Other divisions include INFINITIVE, e.g. *to walk*; e.g. *walking*, or who walks; and IMPERATIVE, e.g. "*walk*....before Me...".

The major Hebrew conjunctions are explained briefly on pp. 44-55, USING YOUNG'S CONCORDANCE. (Refer to "Workshop Example" in *Description of The Book* in this chapter, and also in this text, Chapter Two, **Analytical Concordance to the Holy Bible**, Robert Young).

Hebrew TENSES are defined differently from English tenses, which refer to the TIME at which an action took place.

In Hebrew the tenses refer to whether the action is COMPLETE or INCOMPLETE. In the Concordance these tenses are called Preterite and Future.

PRETERITE (now called PERFECT) tense expresses a complete action or one that is conceived to have been completed an action that is once for all as final, whether past, present or future (e.g. the language of the prophets).

FUTURE (now called IMPERFECT) tense expresses *action not yet completed*, either actually or from the perspective of the writer, what is coming to pass, and future, what is continued and in progress at any point in time -- past, present or future.

For example, of the difference between the two tenses, see Page 1184, No. 7462. Note how the use of the word differs in the KAL Preterite and the KAL future.

Thus, when studying a verb, it is important to recognize the difference between completed and uncompleted action. The **TIME** at which the action takes place is largely determined by the reading of the word in its context!

NEW ENGLISHMAN'S

HEBREW CONCORDANCE

WORKSHOP

TOOLS NEEDED: New Englishman's Hebrew Concordance and Strong's Workshop assignment #4.

ASSIGNMENT: Work through the following directions.

The full benefit of the Hebrew Concordance will not be recognized until the student learns how to utilize it in connection with "word studies" later on in this course. The following workshop will serve primarily to familiarize the student with the Concordance. It is based upon Strong's Workshop assignment #4 and the student should refer to it for the basic information needed below, then look up the following words in your Hebrew Concordance and list all the scripture references for each way the Greek word is translated in the King James' Version.

1.   Proverbs 29:18 - Perish

    A.   Strong's Number -

    B.   Ways Word is Translated -

           *
           *
           *
           *
           *
           *
           *
           *
           *

2.   Psalm 100:4 - Thanksgiving

    A.   Strong's Number -

    B.   Ways Word is Translated -

           *
           *
           *
           *
           *

CHAPTER SIX

THE NEW THAYER'S LEXICON

I. THE PURPOSE OF THE BOOK

The objective of this lexicon is to provide for the serious Bible student a comprehensive understanding of each Greek word used in the New Testament. This is done by discussing the origin and classical usage of each word; by giving an accurate and full definition of it; and by illustrating its applied definitions with references to various verses of Scripture in which it occurs. Because of its thoroughness it is a very important tool for doing "word studies".

II. A DESCRIPTION OF THE BOOK

Introductory Material

The book commences with nineteen pages of introductory material such as, the author's preface, a list of ancient authors quoted or referred to, a list of books referred to, and most importantly, a listing of explanations and abbreviations. To effectively use this lexicon the student should be familiar with pages XVIII and XIX.

A. The Lexicon

A lexicon is a dictionary. This particular dictionary is primarily comprised of an alphabetical listing of words like one would find in a dictionary of English words except these words are listed alphabetically according to the Greek alphabet in Greek characters. In previous editions this meant that only those with at least some knowledge of Greek could use this source. However, this new edition has an added feature that allows the student with no knowledge of Greek the privilege of utilizing it. The numbering system from the Greek dictionary in Strong's Concordance has been incorporated into this text thus making it possible for the non-Greek student to trace any English word in the New Testament to its Greek equivalent in Strong's and then obtain a full analysis of it in Thayer's.

At the top of each page the first word on that page is given in the left corner and the last word in the right corner. Just inside of these are their corresponding Strong's numbers. Down the outside columns are two-digit numbers beside each entry. These naturally fall between the two numbers at the top of the page (e.g. on page 103 the numbers 89, 90, 91, 92, 93 and 94 are actually 989, 990, 991, 992, 993 and 994).

Immediately following each Greek word the student will find technical information such as: different forms of the word, its root word or origin, its varying notation in different manuscripts, its use in the Septuagint, etc. Then follows the basic definition of the word always printed in italics. Many words have more than one simple meaning and these are each dealt with separately under headings consisting of bold print letters and numerals. Most definitions will be illustrated by Scriptural references and substantiated by references to other ancient Greek literature.

This section includes pages 1 to 683.

B.   The Appendix

The book closes with various listings of Greek words to illustrate certain points and some additions and corrections

III.   HOW TO USE THE BOOK

For the non-Greek student the use of this Lexicon is intimately tied with that of the Strong's Concordance. The student will have to use his Strong's to find the number of the Greek word he desires to research. Then he may proceed to find that word in Thayer's and obtain the desired information.

NEW THAYER'S WORKSHOP

assignment #1

TOOLS NEEDED: A Strong's Concordance, a New Thayer's Lexicon and a King James Version of the Bible.

ASSIGNMENT: Read the verses listed below. Look up each word listed in your Strong's to find the number of the corresponding Greek word and write it down. Then look up that word in your New Thayer's Lexicon and answer the questions given. If you have any difficulty raise your hand and an instructor will assist you.

1. Romans 5:10, 21 - **Death**

   How many primary definitions of this word are there?

   Write out the one that is meant in Romans 5:10.

   Write out the one that is meant in Romans 5:21.

2. Romans 12:2 - **Transformed**

   What does this word mean?

   How is it used in relation to Christ?

3. Colossians 1:11 - **Patience, Long-suffering**

   What do these words mean?

   After reading their entire articles, explain the difference between them.

4.   II Timothy 2:5, 24 - **Strive**

What do the two Greek words for strive mean?

How are they different?

How does this solve the apparent contradiction that the minister should strive and not strive at the same time?

NEW THAYER'S WORKSHOP

assignment #2

TOOLS NEEDED: A Strong's Concordance, a New Thayer's Lexicon and a King James Version of the Bible.

ASSIGNMENT: Read the verses below then record the Strong's number for the Greek word behind the word listed. Read through the appropriate article in Thayer's and find the applied definition relating to that specific verse. Write this out along with a statement of what insight into the verse this information gives you.

1.   Acts 2:42 - **Continued**

2.   Romans 15:26 - **Pleased**

3.   I Timothy 4:12 - **Conversation**

4.   Galatians 5:23 - **Temperance**

5.   I Corinthians 6:17 - **Joined**

CHAPTER SEVEN

GESENIUS'
HEBREW LEXICON

(CODED TO STRONG'S CONCORDANCE)

I.   **THE PURPOSE OF THE BOOK**

The objective of this Lexicon is to provide for every serious Bible student a comprehensive understanding of each Hebrew/Chaldee word used in the Old Testament. This is done by often listing the origin and etymology of each word, by giving an accurate and full definition of it, and by illustrating applied definitions with references to various verses of Scripture in which it occurs.

II.   **A DESCRIPTION OF THE BOOK**

Introductory Material

The book commences with fifteen pages of introductory material such as the publisher's introduction, the preface and an address "to the student". To effectively use this lexicon, the student should be particularly familiar with pages v-viii as it contains important explanations.

A.   **The Lexicon**

A lexicon is a dictionary. This particular dictionary is comprised of listing of Hebrew words written in Hebrew characters and arranged alphabetically according to the Hebrew alphabet. In previous editions this meant that only those with some knowledge of the Hebrew language could use this source. However, this new edition has an added feature that allows the student with no knowledge of Hebrew the privilege of utilizing it. This lexicon is now keyed to the Strong's Concordance. This means that the numbering system from the Hebrew dictionary in Strong's Concordance has been incorporated into this text making it possible for the non-Hebrew student to trace any English word in the Old Testament to its Hebrew equivalent in Strong's and then obtain a fuller analysis and definition of it in Gesenius'.

At the top of each page the first Hebrew word on that page is given in the left corner and last word in the right corner. Just inside of these are their corresponding Strong's numbers. Down the outside columns the Strong's numbers are placed beside the appropriate Hebrew word. These numbers will not always be found in numerical order due to some listing differences between Strong and Gesenius. However, any breaks in the numerical sequence are noted with stars, footnotes and dots. Please read pages vii and viii for the full explanation of these and other symbols.

Immediately following each Hebrew word, the student will possibly find its gender (if it is a noun), its part of speech, its Syriac, Arabic or Greek equivalent, and/or its root or some other etymological information.

Following this are the definitions of the word. Verbs carry a primary or root definition which always occurs first and is printed in block letters. This distinguishes it from the secondary or applied definition which follow and are printed in italics. Nouns and other parts of speech are italicized and primary definitions are not emphasized.

This section includes pages 1 to 816.

B.   **Appendix**

The book closes with two indexes. The first is a "Grammatical and Analytical Index" (pp. 877-884) which lists both noun and verb forms from an 1831 edition of Gesenius' Hebrew Grammar. Following this is a much more usable English index (pp. 885-919) that can be used in locating the Hebrew equivalents of English words including even proper names.

III.   **HOW TO USE THE BOOK**

For the non-Hebrew student, the use of this lexicon is intimately tied with that of the Strong's Concordance. The student will have to use his Strong's to find the number of the Hebrew word he desires to research. Then he may proceed to find that word in Gesenius' and obtain the desired information.

GESENIUS' WORKSHOP

assignment #1

TOOLS NEEDED: A Strong's Concordance, a Gesenius' Hebrew Lexicon (keyed to Strong's) and a King James Version of the Bible.

ASSIGNMENT: Read the verses listed below. Look up each word listed in your Strong's to find the number of the corresponding Hebrew word and write it down. Also write down the English transliteration of the word. Using the Strong's number, look up the word in your Gesenius' Lexicon and answer the questions given. If you have any difficulty raise your hand and an instructor will assist you.

1.   Proverbs 23:4 - **Labor**

   A.   Strong's Number -
   B.   Transliteration -

What is the primary definition? (write the full sentence definition)

What is the secondary definition?

Does this verse teach that it is wrong to work for gain? If not, then based on the definition of "labor", what does it mean?

2.   Psalm 21:3,4 - **Preventest**

   A.   Strong's Number -
   B.   Transliteration -

What is the primary definition of this word?

How many definitions are there?

Write the full applied definition that relates to this passage.

What does this verse mean in the light of this information?

3.   Joshua 1:14 - **Armed**

    A.   Strong's Number -
    B.   Transliteration -

What page is this word located on? (Note: It is slightly out of sequence.)

What does it mean?

Applying this to Joshua 1:12-15, what attitude were the Reubenites and Gadites to have toward helping their brethren?

GESENIUS' WORKSHOP

assignment #2

TOOLS NEEDED: A Strong's Concordance, a new (coded) Gesenius' Lexicon, and a King James Version of the Bible.

ASSIGNMENT: Read the verses, listed below. Look up each word(s) listed in your Strong's to find the number of the corresponding Hebrew word, plus their transliteration, then write them down. Look up those numbers in Gesenius' Lexicon, then answer the questions given. If you have difficulty, raise your hand and an instructor will assist you.

1.   Psalm 116:5 - **LORD, GOD**

Which word can indicate plural unity in the Godhead?

Using Strong's concise Hebrew dictionary, from which simple verb did "Lord" (shown above) originate?

2.   Judges 20:34 - **Sore**

What is the primary definition for this word?

Write out the applied definition for its use in Genesis 48:1

Write out the applied definition for its use in Isaiah 29:13

3.   Deuteronomy 7:7 - **Love**
    Deuteronomy 7:9 - **Love**

Write out the primary definitions for these two words.

Explain the differences in meaning according to the contexts in which each are put?

(PROPER NAMES AND CHARACTER REFERENCES)

4.   Genesis 11:22 - **Nahor**
            Jeremiah 8:16 - **(Snorting)**
            Genesis 16:12 - **(Wild) For Ishmael**

Looking at both Strong's and Gesenius' dictionaries, what do these words tell us of the character of those named or referred to? What spiritual lessons can we draw from them.

What does the "onomatopoeic" reference mean in the article in Gesenius' for the word mentioned in Jeremiah 8:16. Look "onomatopoeia" up in a dictionary first if necessary, and refer to the transliteration of the Hebrew word.

CHAPTER EIGHT

VINE'S EXPOSITORY DICTIONARY

I.   THE PURPOSE OF THE BOOK

As an English dictionary of Greek words this book allows the person with no knowledge of greek to discover the Greek words (and their definitions) that are translated by each English word in the King James' Version of the New Testament. This service, combined with its condensed format makes it a handy "quick reference" tool for all Bible students.

One objective of this dictionary is to give simple, yet comprehensive, information concerning the origin, definition and use of the Greek words of the New Testament. Thus, it can be very helpful to the student involved in word studies.

As an expository dictionary, applied definitions are often given in relation to specific verses of Scripture. If a student is puzzled by a certain word in a verse he is studying he will possibly find a statement in Vine's concerning the meaning of that word in relation to that particular verse. This will provide valuable insight into the meaning of the verse being studied. Thus, this text can also be helpful in Bible exposition.

This book provides not only a listing of all the Greek words translated by one English word but also a listing of all English words used to translate each Greek word. This information will be helpful in breaking the translation barrier.

Acting as a Greek concordance this dictionary will often list all the references in the New Testament where a certain Greek word is used. When the references are too numerous, only those felt most important and representative have been included. This feature will on many cases eliminate the need to consult a Greek concordance.

II.   A DESCRIPTION OF THE BOOK

Foreword and Preface

In these few pages are contained some general introductory and explanatory notes. The student will find here some interesting information illustrating the value of this text.

A.   The Dictionary

This volume was originally published in four volumes, thus the page numberings are in four sequences. All the English words of the Kings James' New Testament are listed in alphabetical order. The alphabetical page headings allow the student quick access to the word he desires.

Each entry in the dictionary is headed by the word being considered along with some alternate forms (cf. page 11; ABILITY, ABLE). Under this title are given certain subtitles when there is more than one Greek word dealt with (e.g. on pages 11-13, A. NOUNS, B. VERBS, C. ADJECTIVES). These subtitles divide the Greek words according to their various forms. Each Greek word is given first in its transliterated form (e.g. page 11; 1. DUNAMIS), followed by its Greek spelling in parenthesis (   ). The entry proceeds to give the word's basic definition, its origin, its applied definitions in different circumstances and references where it is used in the New Testament. Some entries will include all the references in which that word occurs. In this case, the entry will be concluded with the following sign (¶). At the close of the discussion of each Greek word all the other English words used to translate it are listed for further reference work (e.g. at the bottom of page 12; "see ENOUGH, SUFFICIENT").

B.   The Index

The book concludes with an index listing all the Greek words with their English translations.

III.   HOW TO USE THE BOOK

The basic procedure to follow in using this book will be to choose a word out of the King James' New Testament, look it up in the dictionary and extract the needed information. If a word's meaning in a certain verse is desired, the student should scan the entry for that reference. For further study, the related words at the close of each entry can be pursued.

NOTE: Newer editions of Vine's also include some Hebrew helps.

Also the newer editions of Vine's including both Old and New Testament words are keyed to Strong's numbering system. This text is recommended to the student's library.

NOTE: The **Theological Dictionary of the New Testament** is another text of great value in the same field as Vine's Dictionary.

This volume is a one volume abridgement of the ten volume work by the same name; it is thus known affectionately as "LITTLE KITTEL".

A purpose of the book is to provide the English reader with clearer understanding of the original meanings to the THEOLOGICALLY SIGNIFICANT Greek words of the New Testament.

This is done by discussing the "word's secular Greek background; its role in the Old Testament, both in the Hebrew and the Septuagint texts; its usage in such sources as Philo, Josephus, the pseudographical and rabbinical literature; and finally its varied uses in the New Testament and, where pertinent, in the Apostolic Fathers." (p.vii).

However many of the contributors to this volume are from the Radical, Higher Critical, Neo-Orthodox School for Theology and some conclusions cannot be endorsed by the author of this text.

VINE'S WORKSHOP

assignment #1

TOOLS NEEDED: Vine's Expository Dictionary of New Testament words.

ASSIGNMENT: Locate the following words and their Greek counterpart(s) in the dictionary. Write all the transliterated forms next to the word. Pronounce the word yourself and read its definition.

        EXAMPLE: obey - hupakoe, hupotage, hupakouo, peitho, peitharcheo, apeitheo, hupekoos

1. **love –**

2. **hate –**

3. **patience –**

4. **peace –**

5. **heart –**

6. **mind –**

7. **renewing –**

8. **thanksgiving –**

9. **know –**

10. **disciple –**

VINES WORKSHOP

assignment #2

TOOLS NEEDED: A King James Bible and Vine's Expository Dictionary.

ASSIGNMENT: Work through the following directions filling in the required information.

Your Vine's Expository Dictionary can be used to aid greatly your understanding not only of words and their meanings, but also of the meaning of many verses of Scripture. Look up each of the following verses of Scripture. Then give the following information about the word chosen out of each verse: (1) the transliteration, (2) the basic definition, (3) the applied definition and (4) what this information tells you about the meaning of that verse.

John 14:16 - "Comforter"

1.

2.

3.

4.

II Timothy 4:8 - "crown"

1.

2.

3.

4.

I Peter 1:7 - "trial"

1.

2.

3.

4.

CHAPTER NINE

OLD TESTAMENT WORD STUDIES

I.   **THE PURPOSE OF THE BOOK**

This volume is an English dictionary of Hebrew words used in the King James Version of the Old Testament; just as Vine's is for the Greek language in the New Testament. It provides a tool for the person with no working knowledge of the Hebrew language.

A purpose of the book is to provide the English reader with clearer understanding of the original meanings to the Hebrew words translated by each English word. As English has many words, synonymous in meaning, so the Hebrew language also has different words that were translated into the same English word. This work takes each of the English word and lists the several Hebrew words from which it was translated. This feature provides the reader with several aspects and emphasis found in each word he studies.

With the definitions of words, a language consists also of grammatical tenses in the usage of verbs; i.e., past, present, future. The book lists many of these tense distinctions for the interested student. This can help a person gain a greater understanding of time reference and emphasis in a given passage.

There are also times a word in the Hebrew language gains a somewhat different meaning when it is used with other words or in certain grammatical structures. This book notes some of these in the Lexicon sections on each word and helps explain wording that could seem awkward without this understanding.

A further purpose of this work is to provide a concordance listing of the Hebrew words. It was not made to give every listing for each Hebrew word, but the listings in which the words are translated to the English word in consideration. Where there are very few references, they are added into the explanatory paragraph of that word. Where there are more numerous listings they are given at the end of each English word section. Where there are far too many references to look at, the author has listed only those felt significant and worthwhile to the study.

The dual nature of this book as a dictionary and concordance makes it a valuable and easy-to-work-with study aid. In many places it will give all that is sufficient for a student to use and gain a clear understanding of the area he is researching.

II.   **A DESCRIPTION OF THE BOOK**

The Preface

In the preface is explained the purpose and development of this work. The author gives some history as to the creation of this final edition. Also, there are listings and explanations of several Lexigraphical works used in background work on the words.

A.   **The Sketch of the Construction of Hebrew**

Here in a brief way are given the basics of the Hebrew grammar. It familiarizes the student with verb tenses and structures. It is helpful information for greater benefit of this volume as well as further study aids.

B.   Lexicon and Concordance

This section takes each of the English words from the Old Testament, with the exception of proper names, and lists them in alphabetical order. Following each word are listed and defined the Hebrew words from which the English was translated. These Hebrew words are arranged numerically according to their sequence in the Hebrew alphabet. Each one is defined, and when important, extra textual information is given. Following the definitions is a listing of scriptural references using these Hebrew words and each is number coded to correspond with its related word.

C.   The Index

The index lists all of the Hebrew words used in the text. Its purpose is to list the alternate English translations of that word. Each of the alternatives is number coded to show the frequency of that translation in the text. This section is very important to the diligent student. Upon looking at the corresponding sections for each of the alternative translations, a person may gain a wider understanding of meaning and greater listing of references.

III.   HOW TO USE THE BOOK

The basic procedure to use the book is to choose a word out of the King James Old Testament, look it up in the Lexicon section and extract what information is needed. If a certain verse is in question, check for its listing in the references and then read the section on its related Hebrew word. For further use, the alternate renderings for the Hebrew word can be found in the index and each of these studied in their corresponding sections of the book.

OLD TESTAMENT WORD STUDIES WORKSHOP

TOOLS NEEDED: Old Testament Word Studies and King James Version of the Bible.

ASSIGNMENT: Work through the following instructions. If there are any questions raise your hand and ask the teacher.

There are two basic uses for the Old Testament Word Study book:

1.   To obtain a clearer definition of a singular word in a verse as found in the original language.

2.   Doing a topical study of an English word throughout the Old Testament.

These two functions will now be viewed in their respective order:

1.   If a person reads through Isaiah 40:31 it says, "But they that wait upon the Lord shall renew their strength..."   In doing this a person may ask what the word "wait" means. To find out turn in the Word Study book to the alphabetical listing of the word "wait", (this is found on page 470). Then look through the listings of Scripture references at the end of the section and find Isaiah 40:31. Directly behind the listing is found the number "14". The number "14" is the number of the corresponding Hebrew word that is used in this verse. The reader then goes to word "14" and reads, "to hope strongly, to trust, implying firmness and constancy of mind..." After reading through the section on this word the person will then have a clearer idea of what Isaiah meant by "waiting on the Lord" in this verse.

    A.   Do the above procedure for the word "learn" in Deuteronomy 4:10.

        1.   Word Number -

        2.   Definition -

    B.   Do the above procedure for the word "bitter" in II Kings 14:26.

        1.   Word Number -

        2.   Definition -

2. If a person desires to know the overall teaching of a word or topic in the Old Testament, the following procedure is to be followed. Choose the topic or word to be studied and turn to that corresponding section in the book. If for example the word picked was "accursed", the reader would turn to this section on page 5. In observing this section it is seen that there are two main Hebrew words translated "accursed". The reader then begins with word #1 and writes down its definition: "see destroy, Hiphil, to make devoted or accursed..." Following the definition one goes through the listing of Scripture references and finds all those followed by the number 1, corresponding to the first Hebrew word in the section. These are then listed, looked up in the Bible, and any aspects of that topic found in the verse should be recorded.

Joshua	6:17	
	6:18	
	7:1	(All applicable facts and information
	7:11	should be recorded behind its
	7:12	respective verse.)
	7:13	
	7:15	
	22:20	
I Chronicles	2:7	

When this is completed, go on to the second Hebrew word. Write down the definition and then list all the references followed by a number 2. When all of the words have been worked through the study is completed. The reader then takes all his gathered facts and compiles them so as to see a total picture of how that word is used in the Old Testament.

Repeat the above procedure for the word "oath".

1. _____

    A. Definition -

    B. Reference Listings -

2. _____

    A. Definition -

    B. Reference Listings -

CHAPTER TEN

VINCENT'S WORD STUDIES

I. **THE PURPOSE OF THE BOOK**

Realizing that perfect translation is impossible and that much explanation is needed to transpose full meaning from one language to another, M.R. Vincent has produced this text. It was his aim to give to the non-Greek student the benefit of a knowledge of Greek applied to the New Testament. Using a commentary format he has given information concerning the background, definition and use of Greek words as well as providing insight into how the rules of grammar and syntax affect the meaning of Scripture. The student will find this tool to be helpful in word studies and especially whenever studying specific passages in the New Testament.

II. **A DESCRIPTION OF THE BOOK**

This work has been published in one, two, three and four volume editions, thus making a simple yet thorough description difficult. It is basically a lexical commentary in which key words and phrases of the New Testament are dealt with by chapter and verse.

The work begins with an excellent preface that deserves a careful reading, a list of authors and editions and a list of abbreviations.

The main body of the text follows, occupying over 1,100 pages. The arrangement of this section may present some difficulty in that the books of the New Testament are not dealt with in their customary order but are arranged according to their author. Thus, their order is as follows:

Matthew	I John	Colossians
Mark	II John	Philemon
Luke	III John	I Thessalonians
Acts	Revelation	II Thessalonians
I Peter	Romans	Galatians
II Peter	I Corinthians	I Timothy
Jude	II Corinthians	II Timothy
James	Ephesians	Titus
John	Philippians	Hebrews

It should also be noted that there is an introductory section to each book which does not necessarily immediately precede it but may be found at the beginning of that group of books.

At the top of each page will be found the book and chapter being dealt with on that page. The numbers of the verses being dealt with on that page will be found in their appropriate place at the left-hand margin. Following the verse number and beginning each succeeding paragraph under it are the words or phrases from the King James text being considered. In the four-volume edition these are in bold print while in the condensed editions they are in italics. Next in the listing appears the Greek word(s) in parentheses followed by whatever information the author felt would be valuable to the student. It should be noted that not every verse is dealt with and often the student will be referred to another passage in the book.

This work closes with varying sections, including indexes and footnotes, depending on the edition.

III. HOW TO USE THE BOOK

This work can only be used in connection with the New Testament. The process is simply that of choosing a text in the New Testament and locating it in Vincent's.

VINCENT'S WORKSHOP

TOOLS NEEDED: Volume I of Vincent's Word Studies and a King James Version of the Bible.

ASSIGNMENT: Using your Vincent's Word Studies research and record the main ideas that you discover on the following passages of Scripture.

Matthew 7:3 -

Matthew 26:15 -

II Peter 1:9 -

Luke 10:4 -

CHAPTER ELEVEN

NAVE'S TOPICAL BIBLE

I.   **THE PURPOSE OF THE BOOK**

The purpose of this book is to bring together in cyclopedic form and under familiar headings all that the Bible contains on particular subjects. This was done by analyzing topically every verse and passage in the Bible and then by grouping under suitable headings all the Scriptures relative to the subjects found in the analysis.

The value of this book is that it removes the difficulty involved in finding all that the Bible has to say on any given subject. It may be used as: a commentary of Scripture upon Scripture, a dictionary of names and places, a book of illustrations of most any Biblical truth, a source of unlimited cross-references to any verse, and a topical arrangement of Bible readings. It is obviously of great value in doing topical studies also.

II.   **A DESCRIPTION OF THE BOOK**

The Preface

In this portion of the book the author sets forth his purpose, his method, the advantages of his method, his sources (KJV and RV), and his acknowledgements. Here he explains his cross-reference system, his sub-topics and his index.

A.   **The List of Abbreviations**

In this section the author mentions the various abbreviations that he will be using throughout the book to save time and space. Particular attention should be paid to the version and directional abbreviations which are found at the head and foot of the list respectively.

B.   **The Topical Bible**

This comprises the bulk of the book covering nearly 1,500 pages. In this section are listed alphabetically the persons, places, significant words and subjects of the Bible. At the top of each page will be found the subject(s) which begins and ends that page.

The heading for each topical entry will be found in bold capitalized print. Following this will be a listing of all the Scriptures relative to that subject which are normally classified into sub-topics. Often the Scriptures will be quoted in their entirety. If not they will generally be accompanied by a word or phrase explaining their contents. Most entries will conclude with a list of other related headings in which the student may continue his studies. Important differences in the Revised Version are noted throughout the text.

C.   **The Index**

Though omitted in some editions, the last section of this book is a 150 page index showing the pages and columns in which each verse of Scripture occurs in this work. In that many verses are classified under numerous headings, the student can easily locate them with this index.

To facilitate such an exhaustive work, the author has used several special markings. Particular attention should be paid to the introduction to the index prior to using it effectively.

III.   HOW TO USE THE BOOK

This book is arranged in alphabetical order, and hence, is very simple to use. If you know the general subject that you desire to investigate simply use Nave's in a dictionary fashion. If you do not find the word you desire, try to think of a synonym for the word. To make your study more complete be sure to investigate the suggested related topics at the end of each entry. If you are interested in expounding a given verse of Scripture, begin at the index and refer to all of the references to the passage in question and read all the accompanying Scriptures.

NAVE'S WORKSHOP

TOOLS NEEDED: Nave's Topical Bible

ASSIGNMENT: Look up the following topics in Nave's and answer the accompanying questions.

1. **RISING EARLY**

    a.   On what page is this subject found?

    b.   List the various subheadings under which the Scripture references relating to this topic are classified.

       (1)

       (2)

       (3)

       (4)

       (5)

    c.   To what other entries does this entry direct you and on what pages are they found?

    d.   How many new topics does this second entry suggest?

2. **JESUS, THE CHRIST**

    a.   How many pages does this listing cover?

    b.   How many sub-topics are there?

    c.   On what page is the coming of Christ dealt with?

3. **SHEMAIAH**

    a.   How many men in Scripture were called by this name?

    b.   Which seems to be most prominent in the Bible?

4. **JERICHO**

    a.   Where was the city located?

    b.   What important events took place there?

5. **NAMES AND TITLES OF THE CHURCH**

    a.   Under what heading and on what page(s) can this information be found?

    b.   List the first alternate name mentioned and the last entry with the Scripture verses that include this title.

CHAPTER TWELVE

OXFORD BIBLE ATLAS

I. THE PURPOSE OF THE BOOK

The purpose of this atlas is to provide the student with a basic understanding of the historical and geographical setting of Scripture. The maps are provided to allow the student to locate places visually as well as to discover information relevant to them such as: terrain, vegetation, rainfall, related distances, etc. The text accompanying the maps relates them to the Biblical data, the historical background and the findings of archaeology. Thus, this book is an essential tool in doing "place studies" and may be used in the following ways.

A. The book may be used with any source making reference to Bible places (e.g. the Bible, Bible Encyclopedia, Strong's Concordance, commentaries, books on archaeology, history, etc.)

B. It may also be studied by itself as a brief survey of Biblical history and geography.

C. It may be used as a quick reference source by one careful reading of the Foreword and one survey of the Table of Contents. Thereafter, each place researched may be looked up in the Gazetteer and followed through to map and text.

II. A DESCRIPTION OF THE BOOK

Foreword

The atlas commences with a foreword, table of contents, and a list of abbreviations. These are helpful in familiarizing the student with the book.

Introduction

The introduction consists of a 39-page article entitled, "Israel and The Nations". This provides the student with a comprehensive geographical and historical background. Included are chronological charts and illustrations relevant to the text.

A. Maps and Descriptive Text

This section is the heart of the atlas covering pages 48 to 98. It is divided as follows:

1. **Physical Maps** - showing natural regions, vegetation, rainfall and terrain (p 48-53).

2. **Historical Maps** - illustrating Bible lands in specific periods of Bible history (p 54-91).

3. **Archaeological Maps** - indicating Near Eastern and Palestinian archaeological sites (p 92-98).

B. **Archaeology and the Bible**

This is an elementary article on archaeology which aids the student's understanding of the importance and application of archaeological information. It covers pages 99 to 119.

C. **Gazetteer**

This section is preceded by notes explaining the procedures followed in the Gazetteer and giving the list of abbreviations followed. The Gazetteer proper lists the names of places or regions, the page or pages upon which they may be found in the atlas and where specifically they may be found in the maps listed. This is a valuable help which can save the student much time in using this atlas.

III. **HOW TO USE THE BOOK**

As mentioned previously this book may be studied for itself as a survey of Biblical history and geography. However, its primary use will most likely be to supplement the student's research. Whenever the location and basic information concerning a place is needed the student may turn to the Gazetteer and from there conveniently find the map suitable to his needs.

NOTE: This work, like many, should be used with the understanding that some information in the text, such as dates, tends to follow the opinions of liberal scholars and should not necessarily be assumed to be accurate. This fact in no way nullifies the validity of most of the information given, particularly, that referring to geographical description.

ATLAS WORKSHOP

assignment #1

TOOLS NEEDED: An Oxford Bible Atlas and a King James Version of the Bible.

ASSIGNMENT: Answer the following questions by referring to the physical maps on pages 49 to 41 of your Atlas. If you have any difficulties, raise your hand and an instructor will assist you.

A.   **Natural Regions** (p 49)

    1.   What is the tallest mountain in Palestine?

        What is its elevation?

        How much taller is it than the other mountains?

        (When you have answered these questions, read Psalms 133:3 and Song 4:8.)

    2.   What is the elevation of Jerusalem?

        What is the elevation of Jericho?

        What is the distance between them?

        How does this affect your understanding of Luke 10:30?

B.   **Vegetation** (p 50)

    1.   Is there more forest or desert in Palestine?

        How does this affect your understanding of the phrase "under every green tree" in II Kings 17:9-12?

    2.   What is the predominant type of vegetation in the hill country of Ephraim?

        How does this affect your understanding of II Samuel 18:6-9?

C.   **Rainfall** (p 51)

    1.   Which part of Palestine has the most rainfall?

        Which part has the least?

    2.   Compare the rainfall of the Plain of Sharon with that of the wilderness of Judah. How then is Isaiah 33:9 a judgment from God?

ATLAS WORKSHOP

assignment #2

TOOLS NEEDED: An Oxford Bible Atlas and a King James Version of the Bible.

ASSIGNMENT: Work through the following directions using the historical maps on pages 54 to 91. If you have any difficulties raise your hand and an instructor will assist you.

A.   Answer the following questions using your Bible and the maps and Gazetteer in your atlas.

     1.   How far did Elijah run in I Kings 18:41-46? (Mt. Carmel to Jezreel).

          What was the distance of his journey in I Kings 19:3?

          While fasting forty days how far did he travel in I Kings 19:7,8?

     2.   In the light of Jephthah's rejection, what is significant about the location of Tob? (Judges 11:1-3).

B.   Using your Gazetteer, locate the sixteen places mentioned in Acts 2:9-11.

C.   Write in the following places on the map on the following page.

Areas	Cities	Bodies of Water
Judah	Jerusalem	Dead Sea
Israel	Beersheba	Sea of Galilee
Philistia	Dan	Mediterranean Sea
Amalek	Bethel	Jordan River
Ammon	Shechem	
Moab	Bethlehem	
Edom	Nazareth	
Galilee	Caesarea	
Decapolis	Capernaum	
Samaria		

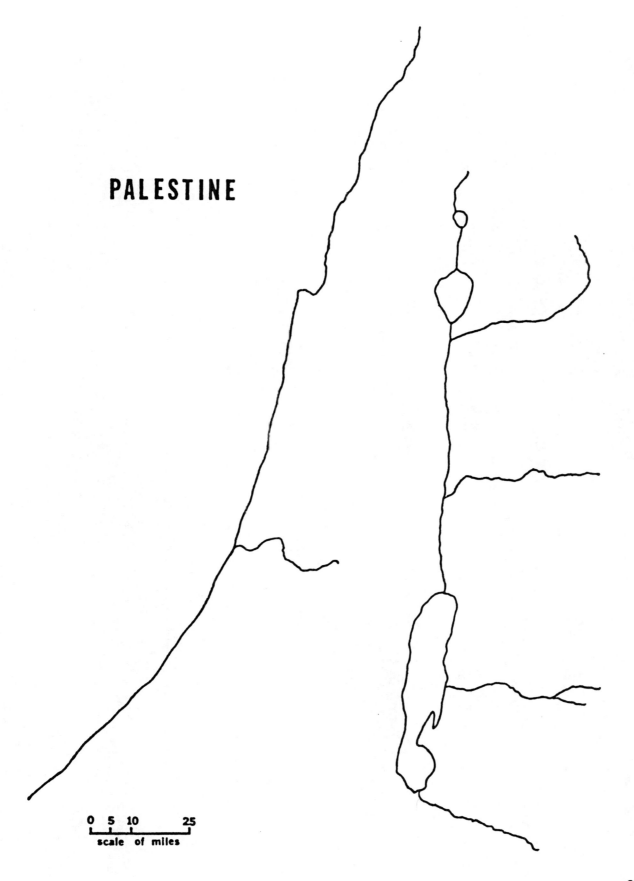

PALESTINE

0 5 10 25
scale of miles

CHAPTER THIRTEEN

UNGER'S BIBLE DICTIONARY

I. **THE PURPOSE OF THE BOOK**

The aim of this book is to provide the student with a concise summary of as wide a range of Bible subjects as possible in one volume. It is not meant to be exhaustive in its treatment of subjects, but rather briefly informative in providing a synopsis of each subject. It is especially helpful when studying persons, places, or things as well as books of the Bible and various doctrines. Perhaps its greatest value is derived from its conciseness.

II. **A DESCRIPTION OF THE BOOK**

Introductory Pages

The first few pages of the book include a preface and a list of abbreviations.

A. **The Dictionary**

This is the bulk of the book covering 1,192 pages. Here most all Biblical and related subjects are listed in alphabetical order to facilitate easy reference. The subjects range from people and places, the geography, history, customs and culture of the Bible lands and times, to clear studies on the great doctrines of the Christian faith, such as Justification, Salvation, Revelation, Inspiration and Holiness. Introductions to each book of the Bible are given. Architecture, styles of dress, plants, birds and animals are included in the many topics, these being illuminated with drawings, charts, maps and photographic illustrations.

B. **Maps**

The text concludes with sixteen colored maps.

III. **HOW TO USE THE BOOK**

The Bible Dictionary should be among the first sources that a student refers to when studying any Bible subject. He will find here a concise treatment of the subject that will not only provide him with a general "over-all" view of the subject, but that also will suggest further avenues of research. The alphabetical arrangement simplifies the use of this text considerably. If a student cannot find his subject, he should think of some synonyms for it and pursue them. Often at the end of an entry the student will be referred to related subjects that will help expand his understanding.

BIBLE DICTIONARY WORKSHOP

TOOLS NEEDED: Unger's Bible Dictionary and a King James Version of the Bible.

ASSIGNMENT: Work through the following directions. If you have any difficulty, raise your hand and an instructor will assist you.

1.   **AN OBJECT – crown** - I Corinthians 9:24-27

What kinds of crowns are referred to in Scripture? What was the crown figurative of?

What light does this shed on the meaning of I Corinthians 9:25?

2.   **A PERSON – Stephen** - Acts 6,7

Who was Stephen?

Why was he arrested?

What was unusual about his martyrdom?

3.   **A PLACE – Bethel** - Amos 5:5

How was Bethel associated with both true and false worship?

What does this name mean?

4.   **A DOCTRINE – Forgiveness**

Write a summary of the Biblical teaching concerning forgiveness.

CHAPTER FOURTEEN

THE INTERNATIONAL STANDARD BIBLE ENCYCLOPEDIA

I.   THE PURPOSE OF THE SET

The purpose of this set of books is to give the student basic information on a great number of Bible and Bible-related subjects. People, places, plants, animals, customs, climate, theological concepts, languages and historical sketches of nations may be found among the topics discussed. The encyclopedia goes even to the extent of including all the distinctly significant words used in Scripture. It brings together in one organized set a wide-range of scholarship on a great variety of Bible subjects, thus making it very useful to the student for most any type of Bible study.

II.   A DESCRIPTION OF THE SET

There has been more than one edition of this five-volume set published, but there is very little difference between them, thus we will deal with the material common to all.

Introductory Pages

This set commences with a preface containing noteworthy introductory material, a list of abbreviations and some helps to English, Hebrew and Greek pronunciation. These pages should be studied to render the use of these volumes more effective.

A.   The Encyclopedia

This is the main body of the work comprising 3,159 pages of well-organized information. The articles are arranged alphabetically for quick reference, and page headings speed the process of location. The title of the article is listed in bold capitals, the main divisions in bold italics, the sub-divisions in cut-in headings and further sub-divisions in plain numerals and letters. This work has a good system of cross-references allowing the student to extend his research into related subjects.

B.   The Indexes

More than half of the last volume is composed of seven indexes (five in some editions). They include: an index of contributors, a general index of subjects, an index of Scripture references, indexes of Hebrew and Greek words and optional indexes of illustrations and maps. If the student familiarizes himself with these, they will prove to be of great benefit to his studies.

III.   HOW TO USE THE SET

There are a wide range of possibilities as to when the student will find this set helpful. This is a good set to consult when studying most any topic. Subjects are easy to locate and are well-divided, so that not much time need be wasted in getting to a specific desired point. If the student is studying a specific verse or word, he may use the indexes to gain helpful information.

INTERNATIONAL STANDARD BIBLE ENCYCLPEDIA
WORKSHOP

TOOLS NEEDED: Volumes I and IV of the International Standard Encyclopedia and a King James Version of the Bible.

ASSIGNMENT: Work through the following directions. If you have any difficulty, raise your hand and an instructor will assist you.

1. **AN OBJECT – Armor** - Ephesians 6:11-17

    Which part of the armor in Ephesians 6:11-17 are mentioned in the Encyclopedia?

2. **A WORD – Advocate** - I John 2:1

    Using your index list the four articles (and page numbers) that relate to this word.

    Look up the word **advocate** and explain its meaning in I John 2:1.

3. **A PERSON – Ahab**

    What does his name mean?

    What were his sins?

    How did he die?

4. **A PLACE – Baca** - Psalm 84:5-7

    After reading the article on Baca in the Encyclopedia explain the meaning of Psalm 84:6.

5. **A DOCTRINE – Baptism**

    How many articles on baptism are there?

    What views do they represent?

    List the other articles that have the word **baptism** in their titles.

CHAPTER FIFTEEN

MANNERS AND CUSTOMS

I. THE PURPOSE OF THE BOOK

In that the Bible was written in an Oriental cultural context there are many hindrances to the western mind being able to fully understand many portions of it. Thus, the purpose of this book is to remove those hindrances by shedding light on the culture of Scripture. As a "Dictionary of things," it is designed to illustrate the Bible by explaining the customs to which it refers. Because of its Scripture text arrangement, it is a good quick-reference tool to use when needing cultural insight.

II. A DESCRIPTION OF THE BOOK

Introductory Page

The first twelve pages of the book are introductory and include a preface, a list of authorities and a list of engravings.

A. Handbook of Bible Manners and Customs

This section comprises the main body of the book covering about 460 pages. There are 893 Scriptural texts that are specifically dealt with. Each is numbered and it is arranged in the order in which it appears in Scripture (Genesis 4:20-21, being the first entry and Revelation 19:12 being the last). On each page, the book being dealt with is listed beside each number. At the beginning of each entry, the Scripture being dealt with is quoted. An explanation of the custom involved follows, accompanied often by cross-references and illustrations.

B. Indexes

The book concludes with these indexes; an analytical index in which all the numbered customs are categorized, a textual index in which all the portions of Scripture referred to in the book are listed and a topical index in which subjects are listed alphabetically.

III. HOW TO USE THE BOOK

This book is very simple to use. If you know the Scripture reference with which you desire help, you can either open to the section in the book that deals with the portion of Scripture, or you can look in the Scripture index in the back of the book under the verse in question. If this verse in question is not listed in the Scripture index, it is not discussed in the book.

If on the other hand you are doing a topical study, it would be helpful to make use of the analytical and topical indexes provided. All of the indexes will point you to the number of the entry in the book (not the page number).

MANNERS AND CUSTOMS WORKSHOP

TOOLS NEEDED: Manners and Customs of the Bible and a King James Version of the Bible.

ASSIGNMENT: Follow the specific instructions for each section and fill in the desired information.

    I.   Using the **Scripture Index**, look up the following Scriptures and

        (1) Write out the verse in full.
        (2) List the entry number(s) relating to that verse.
        (3) Summarize the insight that you gain from your research.

        A.   **LUKE 18:25**

           1.

           2.
           3.

        B.   **MATTHEW 23:5**

           1.

           2.
           3.

        C.   **GENESIS 37:24**

           1.

           2.
           3.

    II.   Using the **Topical Index**, look up the following Scriptures and

        (1) List the number of the entry or entries.
        (2) Read the entire entry.
        (3) List all of the verses which are mentioned in this entry.

(4) Read all of the verse that you have listed.

A.   **SAWING ASUNDER**

B.   **MILLSTONES**

C.   **SWADDLING CLOTHES** (See: Clothes, Swaddling)

CHAPTER SIXTEEN

THEOLOGICAL WORDBOOK OF THE OLD TESTAMENT
(Harris, Archer, Waltke)
Moody Press

I.   **THE PURPOSE OF THE BOOK**

The objective of this lexicon is to provide for every serious Bible student a comprehensive understanding of important Hebrew/Chaldee words used in the Old Testament. This is done by often listing the origin and etymology of each word, by giving an accurate and full definition of it, and by illustrating applied definitions with references to various verses of Scripture in which it occurs.

II.   **A DESCRIPTION OF THE BOOK**

Introductory Material

The work comprises two volumes, but with consecutive page numbering. Both commence with an introduction (pp. iii-v) stating the aim and limitations of the work. Pages vii-viii list the forty-six contributors to the work and the initials by which their contribution is identified in the main body of the lexicon.

"SUGGESTIONS FOR USE", (pp. ix-xiii) is probably only of interest to Hebrew students. "ABBREVIATIONS" (pp. xv-xvii) however, will need consultation frequently.

A.   **The Lexicon**

A lexicon is a dictionary. This particular dictionary is comprised of the listing of Hebrew words in Hebrew alphabetical order, two volumes (pp. 3-982) followed by a listing of Aramaic words in Aramaic alphabetical order (pp. 989-1086).

In the index (Vol. II, pp. 1087-1124), it will be found that this lexicon is keyed to the Strong's Concordance. This means that the numbering system from the Hebrew/Chaldee in Strong's Concordance has been incorporated into this text making it possible for the non-Hebrew student to trace any English word in the Old Testament to its Hebrew/Chaldee equivalent in Strong's and then obtain a fuller analysis and definition of it in Theological Wordbook.

At the top of each double page the first Hebrew word on that page is given in the left corner and last word in the right corner. Just preceding these are their corresponding Wordbook numbers.

The entry studies the word from the viewpoint of Biblical usage, etymological background, comparison with cognate languages, translation in the ancient versions, synonyms, antonyms and theological significance. Also, some consideration is given to words in difficult passages.

The Wordbook collects related words and defines nouns, adjectives and so on, together with the root from which they are derived.

For the non-Hebrew student, the most important aspect of the word is pp. 1087-1124. Page 1087 should be thoroughly digested before using this Wordbook and its instructions followed exactly.

III.   **HOW TO USE THE BOOK** (refer p. 1087)

For the non-Hebrew student, the use of this lexicon is intimately tied with that of the Strong's Concordance.

The student will follow this procedure in his use of the Theological Wordbook of the Old Testament:

Find the word he desires to research and its dictionary number in Strong's Concordance.

Then proceed to the index of the Theological Wordbook of the Old Testament (pp. 1087-1124) and find Strong's corresponding number.

Once the Strong's number is located, then right opposite is the number of the Theological Wordbook of the Old Testament providing the information for the particular word under research.

Example:

The word to study: **Ephod** (Exodus 25:7).
Strong's Dictionary number: S.C. 646.

Index, page 1090 and Strong's corresponding number 646.

Wordbook number right opposite Strong's 646 is 142.la.

Now turn to Wordbook 142 la (page 63) and study the provided information for your word research.

THEOLOGICAL WORDBOOK OF OLD TESTAMENT
WORKSHOP

TOOLS NEEDED: Strong's Concordance, Gesenius (or New Brown-Driver-Briggs), Theological Wordbook of Old Testament, New Englishman's Hebrew Concordance, and a King James Version of the Bible.

ASSIGNMENT: Look up in Strong's the Hebrew word for "perfect" in the verse below. Then apply the proper information under each book below. Using your Hebrew Concordance look up in your Bible every usage of that Hebrew word in the Old Testament. In the columns below write down the references, the ways it is used in those passages, and its topical significance in each passage.

Scripture Reference and word. Job 11:7 - "perfection"

STAGE ONE – Definition

Strong's

A. Dictionary number -

B. Transliteration -

C. Etymology -

D. Definition -

E. Ways translated -

Gesenius

Definition and Information

Theological Wordbook

Dictionary Number and Information

STAGE TWO - Scripture Analysis

Using Englishman's Hebrew/Concordance

Scripture	Usage In Passage Brief Verse Quote and Important Details	Topical Significance/Insights

STAGE THREE - Organization

Using these questions as a guideline, categorize the Scriptures in relation to the word "perfection"

What is perfection?

A.

B.

C.

Who is in perfection?

A.

B.

C.

What are the objects of perfection?

A.   Natural

B.   Spiritual

Section III
METHODS OF RESEARCH

CHAPTER SEVENTEEN

WORD STUDIES

I. **DEFINITION**

Perhaps the most basic method of Bible Study is a word study. In it a student chooses just **one word** from Scripture and proceeds to discover all he can about it. By gaining a comprehensive understanding of that word he then not only better understands the truth it represents but also is more able to understand each verse it is used in (e.g. studying the word "comforter" not only gives the student an understanding of the ever-present ministry of Christ and the Holy Spirit, but also gives tremendous insight into certain New Testament passages.)

II. **IMPORTANCE**

In order to bridge the language gap that exists between our minds and those of the Biblical writers there are **two major parts** of the language that must be studied: (1) **VOCABULARY**, which involves the meanings of the words used in that language; and (2) **GRAMMAR**, which entails the ways the words of the language are put together in order to communicate thoughts and ideas. Word studies focus on the vocabulary of a language and more particularly on the words chosen by God out of each language to comprise the vocabulary of Scripture.

The following is a very brief list of some of these.

A.	Salvation.	II Timothy 3:15; James 1:21.
B.	Life.	John 20:31; Psalm 119:93.
C.	Divine Nature.	II Peter 1:4.
D.	Growth.	I Peter 2:2.
E.	Sanctification.	Psalm 119:9,11.
F.	Peace	Psalm 85:8; 119:165.
G.	Joy.	Jeremiah 15:16; Psalm 1:2.
H.	Guidance.	Psalm 119:105.
I.	Wisdom.	Psalm 119:98.
J.	Faith.	Romans 10:17.

Words are our primary means of expression. They are symbols of communication. Therefore, in order for us to fully understand what the Bible writers were communicating to us in Scripture we must attribute the same definitions and connotations to the words as they did. We must understand what they understood those words to mean. This is complicated by the fact that it is impossible for any English translation to perfectly express the full meaning of the Hebrew and Greek words. One Hebrew or Greek word may be translated by several English words in different contexts. On the other hand one English word may be used to translate several different Hebrew and Greek words.

The words used in Scripture often take on unique Biblical significance. In that they have been chosen by God to communicate truth, they often take on certain divine connotations in Scripture. Thus, a further aim of word studies is to discover what God meant by the words He used, to understand what various words mean in the context of Scripture.

Words are the building blocks of understanding. Therefore, in order to build an understanding of God's Word, you must start at the bottom and build block upon block.

As you give yourself to word studies you will find that themes of truth will begin to open up to you and your understanding of the Word of God will greatly increase.

III. METHOD

There are many ways of doing a word study all of which have their own particular strengths and weaknesses. Some overemphasize certain areas of consideration, some are unreliable as to their conclusions and others are not thorough enough to be of long-term value. If a student is going to take the time and effort to research the meaning and use of a word he should have a method that will not only facilitate a balanced and accurate understanding, but will also preserve his efforts for future reference. The method suggested here is one that is balanced, simple enough for all to use, expandable for greater depth and detail, flexible enough for individual preferences and suitable to long-term use.

Once the student has access to the proper tools, the first step is to choose a word to study. Perhaps the student will have a special area of interest he may desire to pursue. If not, a good starting point is often to take a particular interesting verse of Scripture and study the key word and words in it. If the student is interested in building his understanding of a particular subject or theme in Scripture, he could begin by studying some of its most important words. It is suggested that he start with some of the more central and essential themes of Scripture so as to solidly build his perspective of the truth of God's Word.

By following the three-stage approach as given in the example for the Workshop Assignments the student will discover the joy of word studies.

A. Stage one - Definition

First, all available sources (such as Strong's, Thayer's, Vine's, etc.) should be used to compile the definition of the word. These sources should be noted for future possible reference.

Example:

1. Word - Fellowship

2. Verse - Acts 2:42

3. Strong's -
   a. Number
   b. Transliteration
   c. Etymology

106

    d. Definition
    e. Way translated

4.   Thayer's

5.   Vine's, etc.

B.   **Stage Two - Scriptural Analysis** - Observation/Interpretation/Insights

Second, an analysis should be made using the Englishman's Hebrew and/or Greek Concordance and Bible of how this word is used throughout Scripture. To do so, and to do it properly, every reference should be included.

This can be done in a simple three-column approach: the **left hand** column is used to note down the Scripture reference of each occurrence of the word under study.

Do NOT list the next reference UNTIL the right hand column, where the interpretation or insights are written, is complete. This helps to organize the page and to prevent overcrowding. The **middle** column is used to write out a brief quote from the verse, including the word being studied, or a summary, if that is better. Underline the word for ease of recognition.

The **right hand** column is the one which is used the most. Here the insights which are gained from reading how the word is used and what it means IN ITS CONTEXT are noted. As several points are usually noted, it helps to number each point for later reference.

Turn to p. 110 Word Studies Workshop assignment #1, Stage Two, for an example of this approach.

Once this stage is completed, the student should review the insights written down, looking for natural divisions in order to categorize all references under major headings. This prepares the way for Stage Three.

SC. 2842   SCRIPTURE ANALYSIS   FELLOWSHIP

Scripture Reference	Brief Verse Quote	Topical Significance/Insights
Acts 2:42	Continued steadfastly in the apostles' doctrine, and *fellowship*, breaking of bread, and prayers.	1. Early believers continued in four major areas of church life: 　　a. Doctrine　　b. Fellowship 　　c. Communion　d. Prayers 2. Fellowship included practical care for one another. 3. Etc.

C. Stage Three - Organization For Presentation

Third, a summarization of all the findings and insights should be made, thus bringing the study to a profitable conclusion. The student may organize all the material he has gained by using suitable questions as suggested here:

1. What?

2. Who?

3. Why?

4. When?

5. Where?

6. How?

OVERVIEW DIAGRAM OF A WORD STUDY IN THE THREE-STAGE APPROACH

The following is simply an overview of a word study following the three-stage approach as explained in the previous comments:

WORD STUDY

THREE – STAGE APPROACH		
STAGE ONE	STAGE TWO	STAGE THREE
DEFINITION OF WORD	SCRIPTURAL ANALYSIS	ORGANIZATION/SUMMARIZATION

⇩ ⇩ ⇩

USING THE TOOLS

1. Word : Fellowship

2. Verse : Acts 2:42

STRONG'S
A.
B.
C.
D.
E.
F.
G.
THAYER'S

VINE'S

Etc.

Scripture	Observation	Interpretation
Reference Example:	Usage of Word in passage	Topical Significance
	Phrase in quotes Underline word Note important details	Significance of use of word in verse
		Insights
Acts 2:42	"Continued stedfastly in the apostles doctrine, and fellowship, breaking of bread, and prayers"	Early believers continued in four major areas of church life. 1. Doctrine 2. Fellowship 3. Communion 4. Prayers

Outline from Questions

What?

Who?

Why?

When?

Where?

How?

Summary and Practical Application

Importance of "Context"

In all methods of study, whether Word, Character, Place or Passage studies, the student should constantly maintain the **"context principle"**. That is, he should look at the use of the **word** (whatever it may be) in its **verse context** and **passage context**, discovering where the passage begins and ends in relation to that word under consideration.

Finally, certain guidelines and safeguards should be considered by the student involved in word studies. To be safe in his conclusions, the student should only use Hebrew or Greek words (not English words) for word studies. He should recognize that vocabulary is only part of a language and that word studies alone are insufficient to totally bridge the language gap. Whenever research is done it should be written down, thus preserving the time and effort spent. Finally, the student would do well to be thorough, thus not having to repeat his efforts later.

WORD STUDIES
WORKSHOP

assignment #1

TOOLS NEEDED: Strong's Concordance, New Thayer's Lexicon, Vine's Dictionary, New Englishman's Greek Concordance, and a King James Version of the Bible.

ASSIGNMENT: Look up in Strong's the Greek word for "perfect" in the verse below. Then apply the proper information under each book below. Using your Greek Concordance look up in your Bible every usage of that Greek word in the New Testament. In the columns below write down the references, the ways it is used in those passages, and its topical significance in each passage.

Scripture Reference and word. II Corinthians 13:11 - "perfect"

STAGE ONE - Definition

Strong's

A. Dictionary number -

B. Transliteration -

C. Etymology -

D. Definition -

E. Ways Translated -

Thayer's

Primary definition

A.

B.

C.

Vine's

A. Transliteration (from Strong's) -

B. Definition -

STAGE TWO - Scripture Analysis

Using New Englishman's Greek Concordance

Scripture Reference	Observation - Usage in Passage Brief Verse Quote and Important Details	Interpretation - Topical Significance Insights
Matthew 4:21	James and John "mending their nets" - Jesus calls them	Making complete by bringing each stand back in place and in connection with others - Thus restoring usefulness.

STAGE THREE - Organization

Using these questions as a guideline, categorize the Scriptures in relation to the word "perfect".

What is it to (BE) perfect?

A.

B.

C.

Who is to be perfected?

A.

B.

C.

What are the objects of perfection?

A. Natural

B. Spiritual

WORD STUDIES
WORKSHOP

assignment #2

TOOLS NEEDED: Strong's Concordance, New Thayer's Lexicon, Vine's Dictionary, New Englishman's Greek Concordance, and a King James Version of the Bible.

ASSIGNMENT: Look up in Strong's the Greek word for "fellowship" in the verse below. Then supply the proper information under each book below. Using your Greek Concordance look up in your Bible every usage of that Geek word in the New Testament. In the columns below write down the references, the ways it is used in those passages, and its topical significance in each passage.

Scripture Reference and word. Acts 2:42 - "Fellowship" (SC 2842)

STAGE ONE - Definition

(To study this word fully, its three alternate forms should be included. Because of time and space they have been eliminated here. Their numbers are 2841, 2843 and 2844.)

Strong's

A.   Dictionary number -

B.   Transliteration -

C.   Etymology -

D.   Definitions -

E.   Ways translated -

Thayer's Primary Definitions

A.

B.

C.

Vine's

A.   Transliteration (from Strong's) -

B.   Definitions -

   1.

   2.

STAGE TWO - Scripture Analysis

Using New Englishman's Greek Concordance

Scripture Reference	Observation - Usage In Passage. Brief Verse Quote and Important Details	Interpretation - Topical Significance Insights
Acts 2:42	Pentecost - 3,000 converted "continued steadfastly in apostle's doctrine and fellowship, and in breaking of bread and in prayers."	N.T. Believers had continual fellowship that was demonstrated practically - involving teaching, prayer, worship, sharing possessions, visiting each other, resulting in joy, power and growth.

STAGE THREE - Organization

Using these questions as a guide line, categorize the Scriptures in relation to fellowship:

1.   What?

2.   Who?

3.   Why?

4.   Where?

5.   When?

6.   How?

CHAPTER EIGHTEEN

CHARACTER STUDIES

I. **DEFINITION**

Perhaps the most inspiring method of Bible research is character study in which the Bible is studied by considering the lives of the people portrayed in its pages. It is the least academic and most life-oriented means of study. Its benefit is primarily practical rather than doctrinal and thus can be a personally meaningful means of study.

II. **IMPORTANCE**

There seems to be widespread interest in biographies in secular literature. People quickly identify with the joys and sorrows, and the successes and failures of others. They find it easy to learn and draw strength from the lives of others. Thus, it seems quite reasonable that a Christian would be better off reviewing the lives of those who knew God, and especially those of whom the record is inspired by God.

The word "character" comes from a Greek word which means an impress, mark or likeness. It is used of both God and Satan in Scripture. Thus, in any person's life we will either see the likeness of God and the impress of His dealings or the mark and likeness of Satan. Those who served God gave an example we should follow while those who did not set a pattern we should avoid. The New Testament writers found this to be quite valuable and often referred to Old Testament characters as examples (e.g. John 3:14; Acts 7; Romans 4; I Timothy 2:13-14; Hebrews 3, 7, 11; James 5:11, 17-18; II Peter 2:15-16; Jude 11). If the focus of a character study is that person's relationship to God then the benefit we receive will be greater insight into our own relationship with God.

III. **METHOD**

The procedure in a character study can be quite flexible depending on the character and the desired results. However, there are some basic steps that the student would do well to follow in any character study.

There are approximately 2,930 individuals referred to in Scripture. Some of them are only referred to once and others hundreds of times. In choosing a character to study the student should consider the amount of references involved and whether the person is a positive or negative example. It would be wise to begin with characters one is already familiar with and feels somewhat drawn to. There are two cautions in order here. First, be careful not to confuse people who share the same name. (There are 30 Zachariahs, 15 Jonathans, 8 Judases, 7 Marys and 5 Jameses.) Second, be careful to identify the various names that may apply to one individual (such as Peter, Simon and Simeon).

Perhaps the best approach to a character study is asking and answering certain key questions. The following are some suggestions:

A. What is the meaning of the person's name? A name will often represent a person's character, experience or ministry.

B.   What is their ancestral background? What kind of a heritage did they have?

C.   What was the political, religious, and cultural situation of their day? What was their environment like?

D.   What great events took place in their lifetime?

E.   Who were their friends and associates? A person is often known by his friends.

F.   What character traits did they exhibit (both positive and negative)?

G.   What were their failures and successes?

H.   What influence did they have on those around them?

I.   What was their relationship to God like?

J.   What lessons can be drawn from their lives?

Note : It is important that the student not only follow through the Concordance and Bible for the person's name, but such should be noted in its contextual setting, whether verse, passage or chapter and book context.

Note : James P. Boyd's Bible Dictionary is strongly recommended as a resource book for definitions of Bible names, as well as other valuable information.

CHARACTER STUDIES

assignment #1

TOOLS NEEDED: Strong's Concordance, The New Bible Dictionary, International Standard bible Encyclopedia, Volume II, and a King James Version of the Bible.

ASSIGNMENT: Do a character study on Enoch in the Old and New Testament using Hebrews 11:5 as a foundation text. Complete steps as outlined below.

The student should first read the main chapters, or paragraphs in the Bible which deal with the person's life story. This gives a working knowledge of the character being studied. For Enoch they are: Genesis 5:21-24; Hebrews 11:5; and Jude 14, 15.

STAGE ONE:

Using your New Bible Dictionary make notes of the main facts given along with Scripture references.

Name -

Information -

Using your Bible Encyclopedia make notes of the main facts given, along with Scripture references.

Name -

Information -

STAGE TWO:

Using your Strong's and Bible, list Scripture references, their important details and any insights gained concerning the person.

Scripture	Brief Verse Quote and Important Details	Insights

STAGE THREE

Suggested Questions:

Place main thoughts with Scriptures under the most suitable question.

1. What is the person's name?

2. What is the interpretation of the person's name?

    (a) Positive:

    (b) Negative:

3. What is the ancestral background?

4. What is the political, religious or cultural background?

5. What character traits does the person reveal?

    (a) Negative -

    (b) Positive -

        1.
        2.
        3.
        4.
        5.
        6.
        7.

6. What prominent event transpired in the person's life?

7. What spiritual and practical lessons can be applied to the life of the believer from this character study?

        1.
        2.
        3.
        4.
        5.
        6.
        7.

CHARACTER STUDIES WORKSHOP

assignment #2

TOOLS NEEDED: Strong's Concordance, The New Bible Dictionary, International Standard Bible Encyclopedia, Volume II, and a King James Version of the Bible.

ASSIGNMENT: Do a character study on Abel in the Old and New Testament using Hebrews 11:4 as a foundation text. Complete the steps as outlined below.

The student should first read the main chapters, or paragraphs in the Bible which deal with the person's life story. This gives a working knowledge of the character being studied. For Abel they are: Genesis 4, Matthew 23:35; and Hebrews 11:4.

STAGE ONE:

Using your New Bible Dictionary make notes of the main facts given along with Scripture references.

        Name -

        Information -

Using your Bible Encyclopedia make notes of the main facts given, along with Scripture references.

        Name -

        Information -

STAGE TWO:

Using your Strong's and Bible, list Scripture references, their important details and any insights gained concerning the person.

Scripture	Brief Verse Quote and Important Details	Insights

STAGE THREE

Suggested Questions:

Place main thoughts with Scriptures under the most suitable question.

1.   What is the person's name?

2.   What is the interpretation of the person's name?

   (a)   Positive:

   (b)   Negative:

3.   What is the ancestral background?

4.   What is the political, religious or cultural background?

5.   What character traits does the person reveal?
   (a)   Negative -

   (b)   Positive -

              1.

              2.

              3.

              4.

              5.

              6.

              7.

6.   What prominent event transpired in the person's life?

7.   What spiritual and practical lessons can be applied to the life of the believer from this character study?

              1.

              2.

              3.

              4.

              5.

              6.

              7.

CHAPTER NINETEEN

PLACE STUDIES

I.   **DEFINITION**

One of the most foundational methods of Bible research is place studies. With this method all the various places mentioned in Scripture can be researched. These may include land forms such as mountains, valleys and plains; bodies of water such as seas, lakes and rivers; types of vegetation such as forest, grasslands and desert; and population groupings such as nations, provinces and cities. The aim of this kind of study is to discover a place's geographical and historical significance as well as its possible prophetic and symbolic significance.

II. **IMPORTANCE**

One cannot study Scripture very long before he realizes that the Bible is historically oriented. The twenty-two historical books are plainly so and the others more indirectly. This is because the focus in Scripture is on the fulfillment of God's heavenly purpose on earth. It depicts God's involvement in human history. In that history revolves primarily around people and places, it should be evident that places are constantly interwoven in the tapestry of Scriptural revelation. They have a prominent position in historical accounts, are often in the focus of Biblical prophecy and are even to be found having significance in poetry and doctrine. For example, much of Bible history is centered around Jerusalem, which is also the subject of much prophecy, has a special place in the Psalms and even has significance in the doctrinal books of Galatians and Hebrews. Thus place studies are foundational to coming to a full understanding of Scriptural teaching.

III. **METHOD**

As with other types of study the procedure for place studies is somewhat flexible but should contain certain basic areas of consideration. In selecting a place to research the student should generally allow his choice to arise out of his Bible reading or study, thus complementing them. However, some places in Scripture make good topical studies on their own (e.g. Jerusalem, Mt. Zion, Judah, Babylon, Jordan River, Egypt, Bethel, etc.)

The basic procedure is as follows:

A.   List the name of the place and its meaning. Most places have their name for a certain reason, thus the meaning can be significant. Be careful not to confuse two places with the same name and to identify other names for the same place. (Refer to Boyd's Bible Dictionary of Names, etc.)

B.   Using a map note what kind of a place it is (city, mountain, nation, etc.) and what its location is.

C.   Using a concordance discover how often it is referred to in Scripture.

D.   Accumulate information from your Bible dictionary, Bible Encyclopedia and from all of its references in Scripture (using your concordance and Bible). This should be done with the following four areas in mind:

1. **Geographical Significance** - Gather basic geographical information concerning the place such as: location, terrain, climate, vegetation, etc.

2. **Historical Significance** - Determine the role that place played in the events of history by tracing it through the Biblical record.

3. **Symbolic Significance** - Discover any possible figurative or representative usage of the place in Scripture.

4. **Prophetic Significance** - Locate any prophecy concerning the place and determine whether it has been or is yet to be fulfilled.

5. **Spiritual Significance** - Discover what spiritual and practical lessons can be learned and applied to believers and churches today.

Note :   It is important once again in using the three-column approach as in the Workshop Assignment that the context principle be used in noting the use of the name of the place. The name and its use must be seen in its verse, passage, chapter and book context.

PLACE STUDIES WORKSHOP

assignment #1

TOOLS NEEDED: Strong's Concordance, Bible Dictionary, Oxford Bible Atlas, International Standard Bible Encyclopedia, Volume I, and a Kings James Version of the Bible.

ASSIGNMENT: Do a place study on Bethel in the Old Testament using Genesis 31:13 as a foundation text. Complete the steps as listed below.

I. **List the names for Bethel and their meanings.**

Bethel =

=

=

II. **What kind of place is it?**
Locate it on map and fill it
in on a "mini-map" at the right.

III. **How many times is it referred to in Scripture?**_____

IV. **Geographical Significance**

A. Size_____

B. Near or in what other significant place

_____
(country, mountain ranges, etc.)

C. Natural characteristics of the region:
1. Climate

a. Temperature range_____

b. Annual rainfall_____

c. Other information_____
(droughts, wind storms, etc.)

2. Altitude_____

3. Vegetation_____

4. Terrain_____
(hilly, rocky, plain, etc.)

5. Resources_____
(crops, mining, grazing, etc.)

Scripture Information

Scripture	Brief Verse Quote and Important Details	Insights

V.   Historical Significance

Trace the role this place played in history including people, events, etc. Also include significant Scriptural statements about the place.

Endeavor to make important notes in this section which include the following; if possible:

A.   Political (Time Period)

B.   Cultural

    1.   Language_____

    2.   Religion_____

    3.   Morality_____

    4.   Level of civilization_____

    5.   Race of people_____

VI.   Symbolic Significance

What was this place symbolic or representative of?
What did it represent before God? Before the people?

VII.   Prophetic Significance

List any prophetic statements about the place, fulfillment, and whether they have been or are yet to be fulfilled.

VIII.   Spiritual Significance

What spiritual and practical lessons can be learned from a study of this place and applied to our times, to believers and to churches today?

PLACE STUDIES WORKSHOP

assignment #2

TOOLS NEEDED: Strong's Concordance, Bible Dictionary, Oxford Bible Atlas, International Standard Bible Encyclopedia, Volume I, and a King James Version of the Bible.

ASSIGNMENT: Do a place study on Bethlehem in the Old Testament using Genesis 35:19 as a foundation text. Complete the steps as listed below.

I.   **List the names for Bethlehem and their meanings.**

     Bethlehem   =

                     =

                     =

II.   **What kind of place is it?**
Locate it on a map and fill it
on a "mini-map" at the right.

III.   **How many times is it referred to in Scripture?**_____

IV.   **Geographical Significance**

    A.   Size_____

    B.   Near or in what other significant places

        _____
                             (country, mountain ranges, etc.)

    C.   Natural characteristics of the region
        1.   Climate

            a.   Temperature range_____

            b.   Annual rainfall_____

            c.   Other information_____
                                    (droughts, wind storms, etc.)

        2.   Altitude_____

        3.   Vegetation_____

        4.   Terrain_____
                         (hilly, rocky, plain, etc.)

        5.   Resources_____
                         (crops, mining, grazing, etc.)

Scripture Information

Scripture	Brief Verse Quote and Important Details	Insights

V. Historical Significance

Trace the role this place played in history including people, events, etc. Also include significant Scriptural statements about the place.

Endeavor to make important notes in this section which include the following; if possible:

A.   Political (Time Period)

B.   Cultural

    1.   Language_____

    2.   Religion_____

    3.   Morality_____

    4.   Level of civilization_____

    5.   Race of people_____

VI. Symbolic Significance

What was this place symbolic or representative of?
What did it represent before God? Before the people?

VII. Prophetic Significance

List any prophetic statements about the place, fulfillment, and whether they have been or are yet to be fulfilled.

VIII. Spiritual Significance

What spiritual and practical lessons can be learned from a study of this place and applied to our times, to believers and to churches today?

132

CHAPTER TWENTY

TEXTUAL STUDIES

According to Herbert Lockyer in "All About Bible Study" (p.97) it is computed that there are 31,173 verses forming the Bible; that the middle verse in Psalm 118:8; the shortest Old Testament verse is I Chronicles 1:25; and the shortest New Testament verse is John 11:35.

I.   DEFINITION

Textual exposition may be approached in different ways depending on the way a student desires to approach this kind of study. The following approach has been helpful.

Textual Study is the taking of one or two verses that are complete in themselves and breaking open the verse (or verses), making an appropriate outline and using all its components as the foundation on which a total message is prepared.

It is a more difficult method of study and requires greater thought, carefulness of interpretation and creativity in formulating a suitable outline, and then putting "the body of flesh and sinews" on this skeletal framework.

II.   IMPORTANCE AND LIMITATIONS

It is important to recognize the progression in Methods of Bible Study. Word Studies should lead to Textual Studies. Word Studies are a means to an end, not the end in themselves. Textual Studies also are a means to an end. Textual Studies also lead to Passage Studies and finally to Book Studies.

Because the Bible is one harmonious whole, the student needs to constantly keep in mind that he is to work from part whole and whole to part.

The Bible may be likened to a TREE. The tree is one tree, having roots, trunk, two main branches and many other branches off these two main branches, having twigs and leaves. The Bible is a unity, it is one book, yet has many branches.

*   The Study of the whole Bible is viewing the tree as a unit, as whole.

*   The Study of the Testament, Old and New, distinguishes the two main branches of the tree.

*   The Study of a book is the study of a branch on one of the main branches.

*   The Study of a verse (or verses) is like the study of a twig or twigs.

*   The Study of a word is like the study of a leaf, or leaves on a twig.

The leaf (or leaves) is not the whole tree, but must be related to the whole tree, working from the part to the whole and the whole to the part.

Therefore, it is important to know that no one verse of Scripture is the total or full truth on any given subject. The verse (or verses) may be a complete statement in itself, but no one verse contains in itself the complete theology of the Bible. If this is not realized, then the exegete can lead people into false doctrine.

An example of this is seen in the misinterpretation of I Corinthians 15:29, where it speaks of "being baptized for the dead". This is the one and only verse in the whole of the New Testament that speaks of such a custom. To preach on this verse only and use it to justify baptism for those that have died unrepentant violates the whole New Testament teaching on baptism.

Every verse in the New Testament should be considered and only then can the true doctrine of baptism be discovered. In other words, the first principle of Biblical interpretation is the Context Principle. Any textual study and textual exposition must be done in the light of the whole-Bible context, as the topics of Scripture arise out of the whole of Scripture.

The verse must always maintain its association with its passage, chapter, book, testament and Bible context. The Context Principle is the ultimate safe guard for any verse in textual studies. This must always be kept in mind.

III. METHOD

The general procedure in Textual Studies may be as follow:

A. Choose a suitable verse that you are quickened by the Holy Spirit to expound.

B. Make sure that the verse (or verses) is complete in itself i.e., that the sentences are complete in thought, even if it involves two or three verses. Do not just take a part-verse with an incomplete thought out of its context.

C. Realize that the words are inspired of God and that the words themselves are as "seeds" that can be watered by the Spirit and diligent research and can become "a tree" with "branches".

D. Discover the major thought in that verse and make a suitable sermon title out of it.

E. Break open the verse (or verses) and list all the parts of the verse that may lend themselves to exposition and comment.

F. Formulate an outline. The outline ought to wrap itself around the title of your textual message. Outlining is one of the most important yet difficult parts of textual study. Alliteration is a good and challenging way to outline!

Alliteration = "The repetition of the same sound, usually of a consonant, at the beginning of two or more words immediately succeeding each other, or at short intervals, as the repetition of f and g in the following line:

Fields ever Fresh and Groves ever Green."

G. The outline can be likened to the "skeletal framework" or the "framework" of a house you are building.

The greater part now is to put "the body of sinews and flesh" on this skeletal outline, or, to build the house with windows, rooms, pictures, furniture, etc., on the "framework outline".

This is done by supplying additional Scriptures, comments, and/or illustrations as appropriate to the title-subject and parts of the verse under consideration. One needs to beware of **overloading** any one part so as not to end up with an imbalanced message. The student should seek to present a balanced textual message.

H.   Always check in the immediate passage context for information that may help in the exposition of the verse under consideration.

I.   Watch for the possible use of **the law of opposites** in a verse or passage, i.e., "Walk as children of light" has within it **the law of opposites**, which is "Do not walk as children of darkness."

IV.   EXAMPLES

Two examples of Textual Studies are provided here following the procedural steps outlined under Method.

THE LOVE OF GOD

1.   **The Text** - John 3:16.

2.   **Completeness** - This verse is complete in its thought. It has been called "The Gospel in a Nutshell."

3.   **Seed** - Each word (or words) inspired of God is as a "seed" in itself and can be watered by the Spirit to become a "tree with branches."

4.   **Title** - The major thought in this verse and therefore a suitable title is "The Love of God."

5.   **Parts** - The verse may be broken up as to its parts as follows:-

GOD	-
SO LOVED	-
THE WORLD	-
THAT HE GAVE	-
HIS ONLY BEGOTTEN SON	-
THAT WHOSOEVER	-
BELIEVETH IN HIM	-
SHOULD NOT PERISH	-
BUT HAVE EVERLASTING LIFE	-

6.   **Outline, Content, Scriptures, Comments**

THE LOVE OF GOD

1. The Greatest Lover   -   **God.** Sustainer. Creator of Universe. Personhood.

Genesis 1:1; John 1:1-3. Essential attributes of God.

2. The Greatest Love	-	**So Loved.** Moral attributes of God. Love and all the attributes of love. I Corinthians 13.
3. The Object of Love	-	**The World.** Inhabitants of the earth. Not just the cosmos, but people in all nations. Burden for the world. John 17.
4. The Evidence of Love	-	**That He gave.** Love gives. Ephesians 5:1-2; Romans 5:5-8. Gave Him in death for us. Christ died for us. Love gives.
5. The Channel of Love	-	**His only begotten Son.** Not angel, planet or gift. But His only, unique, beloved Son. The dearest to His heart. No longer animals for sacrifice, but His Son. Colossians 1:12-13; Romans 8:32.
6. The Recipients of Love	-	**That Whosoever...None excluded.** All. Christ dies for all. Jew and Gentile. Not willing that any should perish. Not for the predestined, or preselected. Romans 10:12; I Timothy 2:4.
7. The Condition of Love	-	**Believeth in Him.** Love can only be received in faith. God can love all people but they must believe to receive that love. Faith is the channel for the reception of the love of God. John 3:36.
8. The Purpose of Love	-	**Should not perish.** Born in sin. Perish in hell fire. Christ dies to save us. Not willing that any should perish. II Peter 3:9; Matthew 25:46; II Thessalonians 1:9.
9. The Promise of Love	-	**But have everlasting life.** Greatest promise. Not just physical but spiritual, eternal, God life. Romans 6:23; John 5:24; 4:14.

THE TRUE CIRCUMCISION

1.   **The Text** - Philippians 3:3.

2.   **Completeness** - This verse is complete in itself as to its seed thoughts.

3.   **Seed** - Each phrase in this verse is a seed in itself and can be watered unto growth. Seed thoughts are, circumcision, worship, rejoice, no confidence in the flesh.

4.   **Title** - The True Circumcision.

5.   **Parts** - The verse may be broken up as to its parts a follows:-

      * We are the circumcision
      * Which worship God in the spirit
      * And rejoice in Christ Jesus
      * And have no confidence in the flesh

6.   **Outline, Content, Scriptures and Comments** -

THE TRUE CIRCUMCISION

I.   The True Circumcision

      A.   Circumcision of the Flesh

            (i.e., Jews called the Circumcision, the Concision, Gentiles called it the Uncircumcision. Ephesians 2:11-12; Acts 10:45; Romans 3:30; 4:9; Galatians 2:9; Colossians 4:11. Circumcision the sign and seal of the Abrahamic Covenant. Genesis 17. No Israelite or Stranger could eat Passover Lamb without this sign. The national distinction between Israel and Gentiles, Chosen and Unchosen nations. Exodus 12:43-51; 4:24-26; Joshua 5:3; Philippians 3:2.)

      B.   Circumcision of the Spirit

            Of the heart and the spirit since the cross. The internal, not just the external. Romans 2:23-29; 3:1; Colossians 2:11-13; Galatians 6:12-16; Deuteronomy 10:16; 30:6; Jeremiah 4:4.
            The new creation.
            Implicit is the law of opposites as used here.

II.   Characteristics of the True Circumcision

      A.   Worship God in the spirit

            Read John 4:20-24. Worship not at Jerusalem or Samaria but in spirit and in truth. Exodus 34:8; Revelation 4:10; 7:11.
            Not places but a Person. Revelation 11:1-2. Measure the worshippers.

      B.   Rejoicing in Christ Jesus

            Romans 15:17, 14:17; Galatians 6:14; Isaiah 61:10; Jeremiah 15:16; Acts 8:5-8; I Peter 1:8. Not rejoice "in the flesh" - rites, but "in Christ Jesus" -- a Person!

      C.   No confidence in the flesh

            Note "confidence in the flesh" in verses 3, 4 of Philippians 3 and what Paul could have boasted in which he had in the flesh.

            1.   Circumcised the eighth day. Covenant child of Abraham.

2. Of stock of Israel. Chosen nation. Full bred.

3. Of the tribe of Benjamin. First king from this tribe.

4. A Hebrew of the Hebrews - true blood.

5. A Pharisee as regards to the Law. Well taught in the word. Religious.

6. Zealous in persecuting the Church.

7. Blameless as touching the external righteousness of the Law.

Yet he counts all but refuse and loss to Christ as all external righteousness outside of Christ.

TEXTUAL STUDIES WORKSHOP

assignment #1

THE SALVATION OF GOD

TEXT - Isaiah 45:22

The following example in its simplicity is taken from **"All about Bible Study"** (p 98), by Herbert Lockyer.

1.	The Simplicity of Salvation	"Look"
2.	The Sufficiency of Salvation	"Unto Me"
3.	The Personal Aspect of Salvation	"Ye"
4.	The Scope of Salvation	"The ends of the earth"
5.	The Security of Salvation	"I am God"
6.	The Singularity of Salvation	"There is none else"
7.	The Perpetuity of Salvation	"Everlasting" (v. 17)

The student with understanding, creativity and diligence can develop this outline of the text into a great textual message.

ASSIGNMENT:

Take the above textual outline and follow the six basic steps as in the two examples given developing this into a presentable message on **"The Salvation of God"**.

NOTE :   The student is encouraged to purchase textbook(s) that provide SERMON OUTLINES. These provide numerous textual and sermon outlines which can be developed by following Textual Study Procedures.

TEXTUAL STUDIES WORKSHOP

assignment #2

Following the basic procedures as in the examples given, see what kind of outline and message you can develop from the text provided here in this Scripture.

1. The Text - Luke 4:18-19.

2. Completeness? _____

3. Seed Thoughts ? _____

4. Message Title? _____

5. Parts of the Text -

6. Outline, Content, Scripture and Comments

   " _____ "

I.   The _____ of the _____

II. The _____ of the _____

III. The _____ of the _____

     A. _____

     B. _____

     C. _____

     D. _____

     E. _____

     F. _____

IV. The _____ of the _____

140

A. _____

B. _____

C. _____

D. _____

E. _____

F. _____

Provide illustrations from the Gospels suitable to the above.

7. Practical Conclusions: _____

CHAPTER TWENTY-ONE

TOPICAL STUDIES

I.   **DEFINITION**

Topical studies, also called Thematic Studies, arise out of Word Studies. Word Studies are actually preparatory to and become the foundation for Topical Studies.

In comparison to word studies, topical studies are much broader. Whereas a word study is focused on just one Hebrew or Greek word in Scripture, a topical study views an entire Biblical subject often including many Hebrew and Greek words. Topical studies are the extensions of word studies and building blocks of major doctrinal subjects. They are a necessary step in the process of coming to a comprehensive knowledge of the truth of Scripture. Studying thoroughly an entire theme in Scripture, though often an awesome task is actually tremendously rewarding. By doing so, a student adds a whole new dimension to his knowledge of truth.

A Topical Study is the result of the kind of research that takes a Bible subject and follows it through the Scripture in all its related parts.

Hermeneutically speaking, it is the application of:

A.   The First Mention Principle,

B.   The Progressive Mention Principle,

C.   The Comparative Mention Principle,

D.   The Complete Mention Principle,

E.   The Context Principle.

II.   **IMPORTANCE**

The Bible, though a compilation of sixty-six books, is actually one book. It has unity of thought and purpose as well as progressive unfolding of truth from beginning to end. The truths of Scripture are like rivers that run throughout Scripture, most of them beginning in Genesis and emptying into Revelation, the sea of fulfillment.

Solomon, "the preacher," said, "All the rivers run into the sea; yet the sea is not full..." (Ecclesiastes 1:7).

So we may say, all the rivers of truth, the topics of Divine revelation, which begin in Genesis, run through the Scriptures into the sea of fulfillment, the Book of Revelation. From there they return to God who originated all things.

The Topical Method of study follows "the river" from its inception and origin through its on-flowing to its completion in "the sea". Thus to fully understand any subject, these streams of thought must be traced through their progressive unfolding.

Many Bible students develop a very narrow perspective of Scripture by concentrating their efforts on studying specific verses of Scripture. This is indeed a valuable practice, but it must be balanced with methods of study that give an understanding of what the whole Scripture is teaching. Studying favorite verses at random may be beneficial, but the insights gained must be submitted to the whole of Scriptural teaching on those subjects in order to avoid error from lack of balanced perspective. To understand the Biblical viewpoint of any subject, all the Scripture relevant to that subject must be considered. This can be done through topical studies.

Topical or Thematic Studies are a "Master Key" in the opening of the Scriptures and a fuller understanding of the same. The more the student does this, the greater will be his ability to move into PASSAGE and BOOK Studies.

III.   METHODS

There are different ways of doing a topical study. Perhaps the easiest is by using a Topical Bible in which someone has already topically analyzed Scripture. This is to be favored when the student desires a quick run-down on the subject. The weaknesses of it are a lack of thoroughness, accuracy, definitiveness, and personal analysis based on one's own understanding of truth. The method set forth here is strong in these areas of weakness, and thus, is to be used apart from the Topical Bible.

Single words seldom comprise the fullness of a Biblical subject. Usually there will be several Hebrew and Greek words that are so related on the subject that they must be studied together as a topic.

(e.g., "Sin" is mentioned numerous times in the Scriptures. However, the study of the topic of SIN would involve related words, such a "Transgression, Iniquity, Lawlessness, Error, Unrighteousness" and so forth, in order to get the total Biblical revelation of this theme. It would also include study as to the Origin of Sin in the human race. There are nine Greek words in the New Testament for "sin".)

(e.g., "The Living God" is used about fifteen times in the Testaments combined. However, one cannot obtain the total Biblical revelation of GOD from this one phrase. This belongs to Thematic Study. Hence the need to study "GOD" as to His Nature, His Being, His Essential and Moral Attributes, Character and Power, in relation to the universe and all creatures in order to obtain the whole Biblical revelation on the Doctrine of God.)

Thus word studies are actually preparatory to topical studies and topical studies are actually the compilation of word studies.

The procedure to follow for Topical Studies is:

A.   Choose the word(s) which comprises the Topic. Remember that a single word is seldom an adequate guide to a Biblical truth.

B.   It is important always to make sure you do "Word Studies" and get the proper meaning of words.

    1.   English Translations are often very inadequate to express exactly what the Hebrew thought or Greek word and thought may be as to its contextual usage. Use the Tools for bridging this gap, as noted in previous lessons.

2. In studying a New Testament word, do not forget the use of Old Testament words, for, numerous words in the Greek New Testament have their origin and chief source of thought for understanding in the Old Testament Hebrew background - not the Greek Culture! Remember, the New Testament writers, though they wrote in the Greek language, were Hebrew believers, Hebrew in thought, believing Jews.

3. Some words, consistently translated, maintain their basic meaning in both Old and New Testaments. (i.e., Leaven.)

C. The context of a verse, passage, chapter, book and Testament, or the whole-of-the-Bible context often determines the meaning of the words in a Topic and therefore needs to be checked out.

Check every word in every verse in its contextual use in order to arrive at the full truth on that subject.
What is that verse saying in its use of that word?

(e.g., In the Topic of "Baptism", Word Studies should be combined with Topical Studies in order to come to the complete Biblical truth on that subject. What the Bible, especially the New Testament Books, says on baptism needs to be brought together, compared, interpreted and obeyed, i.e., What do the Gospels, the Acts and the Epistles say about "Baptism"? The Gospels cannot, should not, be used against the Acts, nor the Acts against the Epistles, etc.)

D. Bring all of the research together in a summarization of the Topic. The student will have to gauge the depth and extent of this kind of study according to his own desires and needs. He will be tempted to get side-tracked into many tributaries of thought and related subjects, but he would do well to stick to the mainstream of his subject until finished and then go back and pursue the other areas.

E. After gathering all the information on the study topic, the same questions, given as a guideline under Word Studies, may be applied, as appropriate, here. After columnizing the Scripture references, the theme, major thoughts, then move to the second stage of "framework" using all or any of the following questions.

Who? What? Why? When? Where? How?

There are thousands of themes (topics) in Scripture, which begin in Genesis, the seed book of the Bible, and run through each book of the Bible into the book of Revelation. To discover these in their completeness, the Topical Method of Study would have to be utilized. The Topical Method of study yields a gold mine of truth from these things.

Following is but a very brief list of topics and Bible themes that can be studied throughout the Scripture. It will be seen that Word and Topical Studies are involved here.

Fear of God	The Blood	The Name of God
Love of God	Baptism	Salvation
Faith	Redemption	God
Grace	Reconciliation	Hell
Repentance	Sanctification	Christ Jesus
Holiness	Hope	Holy Spirit
Peace	Jerusalem	Music and Worship
Gospel	New Birth	Feasts of the Lord
Mercy	Power	Truth
Tabernacle of Moses	The Cherubim	Sin
Tabernacle of David	Angels	Satan and Demonology
River of God	Sun, Moon and Stars	Significance of Bible Numbers
The Serpent	The Rock/Stone	Seed of Abraham
Temple of Solomon	Antichrist	Zion

Recommended Textbook: **The New Topical Textbook**
David A. Reed (Oliphants Ltd., London).

146

TOPICAL STUDIES WORKSHOP

assignment # 1

TOOLS NEEDED: Strong's Concordance, New Thayer's Lexicon, Vine's Dictionary, New Englishman's Greek Concordance and a King James Version of the Bible.

ASSIGNMENT: Do a topical study on "patience" in the New Testament. Complete the following steps. (Read all of the following instructions before beginning.)

1. Look up the word "patience" and "patient" in Strong's. Record all of the different numbers (N.T.) for the Greek words translated "patience".

2. There are four main words for "patience" listed there. Do a word study on each of these four, combining their related forms with them. (e.g., 5281 and 5287 belong together.) Begin with the largest number and work to the smallest.

1._____

Strong's

A. Dictionary number -

B. Transliteration -

C. Etymology -

D. Definitions -

E. Ways translated -

Thayer's

Primary Definitions -

Vine's

A. Transliterated (from Strong's) -

B. Definitions -

Scripture	Usage In Passage Brief Verse Quote and Important Details	Topical Significance/Insights

2._____

Strong's

A.   Dictionary number -
B.   Transliteration -
C.   Etymology -

D.   Definitions -

E.   Ways translated -

Thayer's

Primary Definitions -

Vine's

A.   Transliteration (from Strong's) -

B.   Definitions -

New Englishman's Greek Concordance

Scripture	Usage in Passage Brief Verse Quote and Important Details	Topical Significance/Insights

3. _____

Strong's

A.   Dictionary number -

B.   Transliteration -

C.   Etymology -

D.   Definitions -

E.   Ways translated -

Thayer's

Primary Definitions -

Vine's

A.   Transliteration (from Strong's) -

B.   Definitions -

New Englishman's Greek Concordance

Scripture	Usage in Passage Brief Verse Quote and Important Details	Topical Significance/Insights

4._____

Strong's

A.   Dictionary number -
B.   Transliteration -
C.   Etymology -

D.   Definitions -

E.   Ways translated -

Thayer's

Primary Definitions -

Vine's

A.   Transliteration (from Strong's) -

B.   Definitions -

New Englishman's Greek Concordance

Scripture	Usage in Passage Brief Verse Quote and Important Details	Topical Significance/Insights

On the basis of all that you have learned about "patience" from your studies of these four words, answer the following questions. This should give you a fairly accurate picture of what the New Testament has to say about "patience".

1.   **What** is patience?

2.   **Who** is to be patient?

3.   **When** are we to be patient?

4.   **Under** what circumstances are we to be patient?

5.   **Why** do we need patience?

6.   **How** do we get patience?

TOPICAL STUDIES WORKSHOP

assignment #2

TOOLS NEEDED: Strong's Concordance, New Thayer's Lexicon, Vine's Dictionary, New Englishman's Greek Concordance, Old Testament Word Studies and a King James Version of the Bible.

ASSIGNMENT: Do a topical study on "stumbling" in the Bible. Complete the following steps. (Read all of the following instructions before beginning.)

1. Look up the word "stumble" and "stumbled" ("-eth" and "-ing") in Strong's. Record all the different numbers in both Old and New Testaments for the Hebrew and Greek words translated "stumble".

2. There are ten words for "stumble" and "stumbled" listed there. Of these ten words, eight will be used: Hebrew numbers 3782, 5062, 6328, 8058, and the four Greek listings. Do a word study on each of these six words. (Go from the lowest number to the highest.)

1._____

Hebrew

Strong's

A. Dictionary number -

B. Transliteration -

C. Etymology -

D. Definition -

E. Ways translated -

Wilson's

Primary Definitions -

Scripture	Usage In Passage Brief Verse Quote and Important Details	Topical Significance/Insights

2._____

Hebrew

Strong's

A.   Dictionary number -

B.   Transliteration -

C.   Etymology -

D.   Definition -

E.   Ways translated -

Wilson's

Primary Definitions -

Scripture	Usage In Passage Brief Verse Quote and Important Details	Topical Significance/Insights

3._____

Hebrew

Strong's

A.　　Dictionary number -

B.　　Transliteration -

C.　　Etymology -

D.　　Definition -

E.　　Ways translated -

Wilson's

Primary Definitions -

Scripture	Usage In Passage Brief Verse Quote and Important Details	Topical Significance/Insights

4._____

Hebrew

Strong's

    A.   Dictionary number -

    B.   Transliteration -

    C.   Etymology -

    D.   Definition -

    E.   Ways translated -

Wilson's

Primary Definitions -

Scripture	Usage In Passage Brief Verse Quote and Important Details	Topical Significance/Insights

1. _____

Greek

Strong's

    A.   Dictionary number -

    B.   Transliteration -

    C.   Etymology -

    D.   Definitions -

    E.   Ways translated -

Thayer's

    Primary Definitions -

Vine's

    A.   Transliteration (from Strong's) -

    B.   Definitions -

New Englishman's Greek Concordance

Scripture	Usage In Passage Brief Verse Quote and Important Details	Topical Significance/Insights

2._____

Greek

Strong's

A.   Dictionary number -

B.   Transliteration -

C.   Etymology -

D.   Definitions -

E.   Ways translated -

Thayer's

Primary Definitions -

Vine's

A.   Transliteration (from Strong's) -

B.   Definitions -

New Englishman's Greek Concordance

Scripture	Usage In Passage Brief Verse Quote and Important Details	Topical Significance/Insights

3._____

Greek

Strong's

A.   Dictionary number -

B.   Transliteration -

C.   Etymology -

D.   Definitions -

E.   Ways translated -

Thayer's

     Primary Definitions -

Vine's

A.   Transliteration (from Strong's) -

B.   Definitions -

New Englishman's Greek Concordance

Scripture	Usage In Passage Brief Verse Quote and Important Details	Topical Significance/Insights

4._____

Greek

Strong's

A.   Dictionary number -

B.   Transliteration -

C.   Etymology -

D.   Definitions -

E.   Ways translated -

Thayer's

Primary Definitions -

Vine's

A.   Transliteration (from Strong's) -

B.   Definitions -

New Englishman's Greek Concordance

Scripture	Usage In Passage Brief Verse Quote and Important Details	Topical Significance/Insights

WRITE A SUMMARY PARAGRAPH (OR MORE) ON WHAT YOUR RESEARCH HAS SHOWN YOU ON THE WORDS "STUMBLE" AND "STUMBLED"

CHAPTER TWENTY-TWO

PASSAGE STUDIES

I. **DEFINITION**

WORD studies lead to TOPICAL studies. Word and Topical studies can lead one to PASSAGE or Chapter studies.

Passage studies are the selecting of a certain Passage (sometimes chapters) of a Bible Book and exegeting it as to its theme and content, verse by verse. Passage study is expositional study. Passage studies lead ultimately to Book studies.

II. **IMPORTANCE**

The more the student does Word studies and Topical studies, the better skilled he becomes when it comes to Passage studies. Passage studies require the skill of the interpreter and expositor. Passage studies include in themselves Word, Textual, and sometimes Place and Character studies, depending on the content of the passage or chapter under consideration.

In this method of study, the student needs to be sound in Biblical Theology, and sound in Biblical Hermeneutics. The result of these will be sound and wholesome Biblical exegesis or exposition.

III. **METHODS AND QUALIFICATIONS**

Following are some general guidelines that may be used in Passage studies.

A. Choose an appropriate passage or chapter you desire to exegete.

B. The student should make sure that the complete passage is selected, knowing where the passage begins and ends. Many times passages flow from one into the other, but, generally speaking, there are certain themes being dealt with and one can find where these themes begin and end.

   Greek New Testaments, such as Nestle-Arland Text, or George Ricker-Berry's Greek New Testament, show the beginning and ending of certain passages. These can be of great help. However, if one is not knowledgeable of Greek, generally speaking, the change of themes can be discovered by (a) a careful reading of the chapter/book in which the passage is found, and (b) by noting in many translations a paragraph sign, showing generally where a passage begins. (Note: These may not always be exactly correct, but generally speaking they are a safe guide).

   Examples:
   The major theme of Hebrews 11 is FAITH. However, the PASSAGE CONTEXT (using The Context Group of Principles) dealing with the subject of faith would begin in Hebrews 10:19 inclusive to Hebrews 12:2. This includes all the references to faith, not just Chapter 11.

   James Chapter 3 has two major themes, these being, the TONGUE and WISDOM. The tongue is dealt with in 3:1-12. This is a complete passage in itself and would therefore constitute "the passage study". Wisdom is dealt with in 3:13-18. This also is a complete passage in itself to be studied.

Thus it is important to know where a passage begins and ends.

C.   After selecting the Passage, look for a KEY WORD (or words), for this key word generally becomes the "key" to open the passage or chapter.

Examples:

Psalm 150. The "key word" in this chapter is "PRAISE" - used thirteen times in this Psalm.

James 3:1-12. The "key word" in this passage is "TONGUE."

James 3:13-18. The "key word" in this passage is "WISDOM".

Hebrews 10:19-12:2. The "key word" in this whole section (complete passage) is "FAITH".

D.   Once the key word has been discovered (or key thought), this may be used as a suitable Sermon Title. With the above passages as examples we could use the following titles:

Psalm 150 - "A Psalm of Praise."

James 3:1-12 - "The Control of the Tongue."

James 3:13-18 - "Two Kinds of Wisdom."

Hebrews 10:19-12:2 - "Jesus, The Author and Finisher of Faith."

E.   The student should seek to formulate a suitable outline. The use of alliteration is a challenging and creative way of doing this. It helps to make the presentation and reception by the hearers more effective and is very rewarding to the student. (Note: According to Webster's alliteration is "the repetition of the same sound, usually of a consonant, at the beginning of two or more words immediately succeeding each other, or at short intervals".)
Examples:

        The Problem of Sin
        The Power of Sin
        The Presence of Sin
        The Prevention of Sin

The student is referred to Outlining and Outlining Workshop in Bible Research for help in this area.
Outlining a passage for presentation is a very important part of Homiletics, for the speaker "to bring his hearers along with him" in his preaching and teaching and communicating the Word.

F.   The outline becomes "the framework" or "skeleton" which has to be built upon. The exposition of the passage, the supplying of additional and suitable Scriptures, comments, illustrations,etc., then become "the body of sinews and flesh" on the skeletal outline. Congregations do not just want a "bone skeleton" but "flesh and sinews and life of the blood" in the message!

G.   The student should follow the steps outlined in "Methods and Principles of Study".

Observation - "What does the verse/passage say?"

Interpretation -"What does the passage mean?"

Organization - "How can I suitably outline it?

Presentation -"How can I best communicate it?"

Application -"How can the passage/message be applied practically to the people's life-styles?"

Evaluation -"How well did I communicate? Where can I improve?"

IV.   STEPS OF PROCEDURE IN PASSAGE STUDIES

Following are seven recommended steps in doing a passage study in Scripture.

A.   The Passage.

B.   The Key Word(s).

C.   Message Title (from key words or thoughts in passage).

D.   Outline of Passage or Outline of Message from the passage.

E.   Exegesis of Verses/Passages.

F.   Additional Scriptures, Illustrations, etc.

G.   Practical Application and Conclusion.

PASSAGE STUDIES WORKSHOP

assignment #1

TOOLS NEEDED: Strong's Concordance, King James Version of the Bible, and any other recommended "Tools for Research" as required.

ASSIGNMENT: Do a passage study of James 3:13-18 following the recommended steps and suggested outline format as provided here.

1.   Make sure the passage is complete in itself.

2.   Find the key word or words.

3.   Make a suitable Message Title from the key word(s) of theme of the passage.

4.   Formulate a suitable Outline for the Message.

5.   Exegete the verses in the passage. This may involve Word Studies of other Methods of Study as previously done.

6.   Supply additional and suitable scriptures, comments, and illustrations as required (e.g., character studies etc.).

7.   What is the practical application and conclusion of your passage study?

Note: The student may develop the message from the passage study as fully as desired using additional paper.

1.   **The Passage -**

2.   **The Key Word(s) -**

3.   **Message Title -** _____

4.   **Outline of Message -**

5.   **Exegesis of Verses/Passages (only in brief here)**

   A.   Characteristics of _____   _____

1._____

2._____

3._____

4._____

5._____

6._____

7._____

8._____

9._____

10._____

11._____

12._____

B.   Characteristics of_____   _____

1._____

2._____

3._____

4._____

5._____

6._____

7._____

8._____

9._____

10._____

11._____

12._____

6.   Additional Scriptures/Illustrations, etc.

*   **Illustrations** in personal lives, Character Studies.

*   **Additional Scriptures** added where suitable.

7.   Practical Application and Conclusion

PASSAGE STUDIES WORKSHOP

assignment #2

TOOLS NEEDED: Strong's Concordance, King James Version of the Bible, and any other recommended "Tools for Research" as required.

ASSIGNMENT: Do a passage study of Galatians 5:16-26 following the recommended steps on Workshop Assignment #1.

Note: The student may develop the message from the passage study as fully as desired.

1. **The Passage -**

2. **The Key Word(s) -**

3. **Message Title -** _____

4. **Outline of Message -**

5. **Exegesis of Verses/Passages (only in brief here)**

   A. Characteristics of _____   _____

      1. _____
      2. _____
      3. _____
      4. _____
      5. _____
      6. _____
      7. _____
      8. _____
      9. _____
      10. _____
      11. _____
      12. _____

B.   Characteristics of_____   _____

      1._____

      2._____

      3._____

      4._____

      5._____

      6._____

      7._____

      8._____

      9._____

     10._____

     11._____

     12._____

6.   **Additional Scriptures/Illustrations, etc.**

7.   **Practical Application and Conclusion**

CHAPTER TWENTY-THREE

BOOK STUDIES

INTRODUCTION

The study of a Book of the Bible is really the "ultimate" of all methods of Bible study. As Hermeneutics is "a science and an art", the science being "knowing the rules" of interpretation, the art being "using the rules", so Book Study may be said to involve the same. In Book Study, "knowing the tools" and "using the rules" are brought together in order to exegete a Bible Book!

Book Study is often the combination of Word Studies, Character Studies, Place Studies, Textual Studies, Topical Studies, and Passage Studies. It takes the skill of all these methods combined and woven together in order to have sound exposition of a book.

Not every student will be able or called to do this but following are some basic guidelines that one may use to do a Book Study.

I.   **Read the chosen book two or three times** (A.V.), and/or another translation. This familiarizes the student with the contents of the book.

II.   **Define whether the book** is doctrinal, poetical, personal, historical, prophetical or eschatological, i.e., Old Testament or New Testament Survey groupings.
       Note: If the book is doctrinal, especially a New Testament book, then make a brief list of the major doctrines in the book.

III.   **Discover what are the main themes or major theme of the book.** For example Romans has several themes in it but the major theme would be "Justification by Faith". Other themes would be:
       The Divine Purpose in the Setting Aside of the Jewish Nation;
       The Grafting in of the Gentiles;
       The Body of Christ and Gifts in the Body;
       Government by the State, etc.

IV.   **Study the Background of the book.**

       A.   **Time** -When was the book written?
              Note chapter and verse references from the book itself which may indicate the time written. Or, check resource books that may help locate the time of writing within the life span of the author.

       B.   **Place** - Where was the book written?
              Check if any chapter and verse within the book itself gives indication of the place where it was written. If not, refer to some text on Bible Introduction.

V.   **Study the Background of the City.**

       A.   Geographically

       B.   Culturally

C. Politically

D. Historically

E. Religiously - Heathen or Jewish Religion.

VI. Character Studies

A. **The Writer** - Who wrote the book?
Do a character study of the author of the book. Learn what you can about the writer, his personality, his character, either from the book itself, or other books of resource material. Make chapter references as to internal evidence where possible.

B. **The Recipients** - Who were the recipients of the book, or, to whom was the book written? Check internal evidences giving chapter and verse references if there be such. Otherwise, refer to references sources.

C. **Other Persons** - Make a character profile of other prominent persons in the book involved either in the sending of the book or the social setting of the book.

VII. Check the Book for Problem/Solution.

What necessitated the writing of the book? Were there problems that required solutions? Were they church problems, personal problems, national problems, or leadership problems?
Make a list, in brief, from internal evidences of these problems and/or the solution the writer presents.

Examples:

The Problems In Corinth	The Solution of Paul's Writing
Worldly wisdom	Divine wisdom
Carnality	Spirituality
Immorality	Holiness of life
Marriage problems	Marriage order
Disorders at Lord's table	Church order, Table order
Confusion over spiritual gifts	Order of the gifts
Doctrinal confusion over the	Resurrection body and order
Resurrection body	etc.
etc.	

VIII. Old and/or New Testament Connections

A. If an Old Testament book, note its connection with the New Testament and make a list of all the cross-references, allusions, persons or stories referred to in the New Testament. (i.e., Note all the references in the New Testament by Jesus and the apostles from the Book of Genesis.

B. If a New Testament book, do the same as above, making a note and listing all the references, cross-references, allusions, persons or stories referred to from the Old Testament.
It is good to list the Old Testament passages quoted.

(i.e., Note the Old Testament passages Paul refers to in I Corinthians 5, and I Corinthians 10.)

IX.   **Keys to open a Bible.**

The student should look for:

A.   **Key words** - Making a list of them all, and the number of times mentioned, and chapter and verse references.
(It is helpful to refer the **Old Testament and New Testament Survey,** by Conner/Malmin.)

B.   **Key Phrases** - As above.

C.   **Peculiarities** found in the book should be noted, and words or phrases unique to this book only, and needing special study to understand.

(i.e., I Corinthians 15:29 speaks of "baptism for the dead". Only used in this epistle and needing special understanding by study.)

X.   **Outline of the Book**

Outlining the book is of utmost importance as it provides the necessary framework for the exposition of the book.
Suggested guidelines would be the following:

A.   **Title of the Book**
This would be taken from the major theme of the book.
(i.e., Proverbs - "The Book of Wisdom" Romans - "the Book of Justification by Faith").

B.   **Chapter Titles**
These would be taken from the dominant theme in the chapter content(s).

Examples:
James Chapter One - The Believer and Temptation.
James Chapter Two - The Believer and Faith and Works
James Chapter Three - The Believer and The Tongue and Wisdom
James Chapter Four - The Believer and Pride and Humility
James Chapter Five - The Believer and Patience and Prayer

Note: Alliteration is an excellent but challenging approach in outlining!

C.   **Chapter Sections or Sub-Headings**
These will arise out of the following:

1.   Where a subject-section in a chapter begins and ends.

2.   Where the use of the key word(s) in that section is noted.

3.   Where the Greek text (if a New Testament Book) admits the section or sub-section and where one is knowledgeable of the Greek.

D. **Consistent Outline Format** (Refer Sheet)

There are various ways of outlining or format. Whichever is chosen, the outline format should be consistent throughout the exposition of the whole book.

The exposition should basically be as follows:

1. **INTRODUCTION:**

   Dealing with authorship, date, background of the book, recipients, themes, or other related material to introduction.

2. **OUTLINE AND EXPOSITION:**

   The framework and body of the exposition. Includes chapter titles, chapter division and sub-sections of the chapters and verses and exposition of the same.

3. **CONCLUSION:**

   Summarizing the major lessons from the chapter content and exposition.

SUMMARY:

As mentioned in the introduction, Book Study will take the skill of the exegete to weave together the various methods of Biblical Research as worked through in this textbook.

Therefore:

Word Studies
Character Studies
Place Studies
Textual Studies
Topical Studies
Passage Studies
will be woven together in Book Studies!

BIBLE BOOK OUTLINE

The following pages from First Epistle to the Corinthians are just a brief sample outline covering some of the major points and guidelines recommended in Book Studies.

An Outline, Key Words and Chapter Themes page from Chapter One is provided giving ideas for the student to follow.

"CATECHISM WITH CHARISMATIC CORINTHIANS"
(Studies In 1 Corinthians Epistle)

The word "Catechism" refers to a handbook of instruction by the method of "asking questions and correcting the answers". Under the present outpouring of the Holy Spirit there are many questions which have arisen in the "Charismatic Churches".

The Epistle to the Corinthians is Paul's "catechism" - giving answer to many questions that Charismatic believers ask - both then and now!

"Catechism with Charismatic Corinthians" presents an exciting, challenging and stimulating series of studies relevant to the Church of today! Refer to Luke 1:1-4; Acts 18:25; 21:21, 24; Romans 2:18.

Introductory: - 1 Corinthians 1:1-3; 2:1-5.

I.   THE CITY OF CORINTH

A.	It's Name -	**F.**	It's Population -
B.	It's Geography -	**G.**	It's Moral Condition -
C.	It's History	**H.**	It's Religion - Pantheism -
D.	It's Political Status -	**I.**	It's Old Testament 'Church' -
E.	It's Culture - Commerce - Education - Sports - Seaport -	**J.**	It's New Testament 'Church' -

II.   THE EPISTLE TO CORINTH.

It was not until about AD 90 that Paul's letters were collected and put together. It seems that there could have possibly been three Epistles sent to Corinth, of which the Holy Spirit has preserved the major Epistles.

I Corinthians 5:9, "I wrote unto you in an Epistle....."

* The cause for this letter - Corinthians 1:11; 16:17; 7:1.
* Sent possibly by the hand of Timothy from Ephesus - I Corinthians 4:17; 16:10, 11.
* The Epistle of Reproof, or, the Epistle of New Testament Church Order.
* Written by Paul about AD 53-57 during his stay at Ephesus on his third missionary journey (Acts 19).
* Problems in the Charismatic Corinthian Church

A. The Problem of Divisions and Contentions
B. The Problem of Worldly Wisdom and Philosophy
C. The Problem of Carnality and Personalities
D. The Problem of Vanity and Pride
E. The Problem of Incestuous Immorality
F. The Problem of Church Discipline
G. The Problem of Law Suits
H. The Problem of Immorality and Idolatry
I. The Problem of Believers and Unbelievers in Marriage relationships (i.e., Husbands & Wives, Virgins, Widows, Celibacy, etc.)
J. The Problem of Meats offered to Idols
K. The Problem of Paul's Apostolic Authority
L. The Problem of Idolatry, Immorality and Demonology
M. The Problem of Headship & Covering of Men and Women
N. The Problem of Heresies in the Church
O. The Problem of Disorder at the Lord's Table and the Love-Feast
P. The Problem of Discerning the Lord's Body
Q. The Problem of Ignorance concerning Spiritual Gifts, "the charismata"
R. The Problem of the Lack of Love
S. The Problem over the Utterance Gifts of Prophecy, Tongues and Interpretation of Tongues
T. The Problem over the Resurrection Body and the Kingdom of God

The problems noted in the Epistle are evident today in the "Pentecostal/Charismatic Churches". The answers given to these problems are as applicable today as then, if we will listen and obey. The challenge of any Church problem is discovering the Divine Solution!

III. **OUTLINE OF CORINTHIANS**

A. Corrective Section: Carnalities......................1:1 - 8:13
Divisions/Immorality/Marriage/Idolatry

B. Constructive Section: Spiritualities................9:1 - 16:24

Ministry/Communion/Love/Resurrection/
Spiritual Gifts/Body of Christ/Collections

The following SURVEY page of First Corinthians is taken from **New Testament Survey**, by Kevin J. Conner and Ken Malmin.

I CORINTHIANS

1. **TITLES:**

   A. The First Epistle to the Corinthians
   B. The Book of Correction
   C. The Book of N.T. Church Order

2. **AUTHOR:**

   Written by Paul, the apostle to the Gentiles.

3. **DATE:**

   Probably written between 53 and 57 A.D. during Paul's stay at Ephesus on his third missionary journey (Acts 19). Later he visited Corinth again (Acts 20:1, 2).

4. **KEY WORDS:**

   A. Body ———————————————————— 44
   B. Spirit (Greek word) ——————————— 41
   C. Wise (dom, er) ————————————— 31
   D. Tongue (s) ————————————————— 22
   E. Prophet, Prophesy, etc. ————————— 21
   F. Charity, Love (same Greek word) ————— 16

5. **KEY VERSES:** 1:24, 30; 3:10, 11

6. **PURPOSE:**

   A. To answer questions that the Corinthians had addressed to him concerning problems in the church (7:1; 8:1; 12:1; 16:1).
   B. To reprove and correct abuses in the mental, moral, social, and spiritual life of the Corinthian church.

7. **MESSAGE:**

   A. Recognition of the Lordship of Jesus is the solution to division in the body of Christ.
   B. God's church must be built by God's wisdom and power rather than by man's.
   C. To have order in the church we must conform to God's order.
   D. That which edifies the church is sound doctrine and that which motivates the church is God's love.

8. **OUTLINE:**

   I. Corrective Section: Carnalities . . . . 1:1 - 8:13
       Divisions/Immorality/Marriage/Idolatry
   II. Constructive Section: Spiritualities . . . . 9:1 - 16:24
       Ministry/Communion/Spiritual Gifts/Body of Christ
       Love/Resurrection/Collections

9. **SUMMARY:**

   The church at Corinth was founded by Paul, as recorded in Acts 18. It had enjoyed the ministries of Paul, Peter, and Apollos and factions had arisen around these personalities. Other carnalities such as immorality, idolatry, and heresy had arisen. Thus Paul wrote this first epistle to reprove the Corinthians of these and to correct disorders concerning the Lord's Table, spiritual gifts, and the collection. He also answered questions and clarified misunderstandings concerning the resurrection. All of these things are evidence of a lack of spirituality, the essence of which is love.

10. **CHRIST SEEN:**

    Christ is seen as the Power of God (1:24), the Wisdom of God (1:24, 30), our Righteousness, Sanctification, and Redemption (1:30), the Love of God (13), and the Resurrection (15).

CATECHISM WITH CHARISMATIC CORINTHIANS
(Studies in 1 Corinthians Epistle)

OUTLINE OF EPISTLE

I CORINTHIANS

EPISTLE OF NEW TESTAMENT CHURCH ORDER

Corrective Section - Ch. 1-8

1. Divisions
2. Wisdom
3. Carnality
4. Immorality
5. Church Discipline
6. Law Suits
7. Marriage/Celibacy,etc.
8. Idol-Meats

Constructive Section - Ch. 9-16

1. Apostolic Ministry
2. Idolatry
3. Immorality
4. Headship & Covering
5. Heresies
6. Lord's Table
7. Spiritual Gifts
8. Discerning the Body of Christ
9. Love
10. Utterance Gifts
11. Resurrection
12. Collections

CHAPTER ONE

A. Outline of the Chapter

i.   Greetings and Salutations. 1:1-3
ii.   Prayer of Thanksgiving. 1:4-9
iii. Problems of Divisions. 1:10-17a
iv.   The Wisdom of God vs the Wisdom of Man. 1:17b-25
v.   The Calling and Choice of God. 1:25-31

B. Key Words and Chapter Themes

i.   Call, Called, Calling - 1:2, 9,24,26.
ii.   Chosen - 1:27, 28.
iii. Baptize, Baptized - 1:13, 14, 15, 16, 17.
iv.   The Name - vs 1, 2, 3, 4, 7, 9, 10, 13.
      Lord, Jesus Christ, Christ Jesus, Christ, Lord Jesus Christ 20 times + 9 times in total.
v.   The Father and Son - 1:1, 2,3,4,9,18,20,21,24,25,27,28,30.
      Reveals the unity of the Father and the Son in redemptive plan.
vi.   Wisdom, wise - vs 17, 19, 20,21, 22, 24, 26, 27, 30.
vii. Foolish, foolishness - 1:18, 20, 21, 23, 25, 27.

SUMMARY: Those who called and chosen are baptized into the Name of the Father, Son and Holy Spirit, even the Name of the Lord Jesus Christ. these know the wisdom of God in Christ although it is foolishness to the unregenerate world.

BOOK STUDIES

WORKSHOP

TOOLS NEEDED: King James Version of the Bible and any other required "Tools for Research" as in this text.

ASSIGNMENT: The student is to do an outline study of introductory nature of The Epistle of Jude following the steps, questions and format as given here.

Note: By using the tools of research the student will, with their own creative research, be able to produce a suitable framework for a verse by verse exposition of this short Epistle.

1. Read the book through twice in the King James and once in another translation.

2. Define whether the book is doctrinal, personal, eschatological or otherwise.

3. What is the major theme of the book?

4. Who was the writer? What can you find out about him?

5. When was the book written? To whom was it written?

6. What was the main reason for writing the Epistle?

7. What are the key words?

8. What could be the key verse?

9. Make a list of any and all Old Testament references and allusions.

10. Make a suitable outline of the Epistle.

11. Make a list of other important observations in the book.

12. What practical conclusions and lessons for the church may be found in this Epistle for today?

Note: The student is encouraged to do a verse by verse exposition of the book using skillfully the keys given.

CHAPTER TWENTY-FOUR

OUTLINING STUDY

I. **INTRODUCTION**

All the Bible studies should recognize the importance of outlining when it comes to the ministry of the Word, whether preaching or teaching in whatever realm or level.

Outlining requires good skill and creativity. Whatever method of Bible study is being done, whether Word, Character, Place, Textual, Topical, Passage, or Book Studies, outlining is important. Its importance may be seen in the following comments.

A. **Outlining Helps in the Understanding of Scripture**

1. It helps one more readily to comprehend Scripture.

    a. Is the book, chapter or passage a unit, a complete whole?

    b. Or, does it consist of a number of short passages dealing with different subjects?

    c. If so, what are these varying subjects or themes?

2. It helps one to understand the progression of thought that the writer had in mind when writing to his hearers.

B. **Outlining Helps in the Memorization of Scripture**

1. It helps to locate more quickly various passages in the Bible.

2. It helps one to grasp more easily the content of the Bible as a whole.

    a. Alliteration, if possible, sharpens the focus on any book or passage in the Bible.

    b. Sequential outlining helps avoid redundancy.

C. **Outlining Helps in the Presentation of the Scripture**

1. It helps one to present the Scripture message with greater clarity.

2. It helps the hearers more readily to receive and retain the message.

3. It helps to make the subject more interesting.

II. **METHODS OF OUTLINING**

There are various methods of outlining which may be used successfully. The following approach is a general one in this area. It is important to remember that whichever approach is used the student must be consistent in format, whether it be by NOUN, PHRASE or SENTENCE Outlining.

The key to successful study is the ability to organize properly the data that has been acquired. No one wants to be stranded with an endless pile of facts and without any logical method of presentation. For this reason a thorough understanding of proper outlining techniques is most beneficial and time-saving.

An outline is the simplest means of showing the plan of presentation. It is merely a means of grouping similar facts. It should not be a struggle to create, but rather should serve to aid the writer or speaker. Like a builder's blueprint, an outline may be changed as the need arises or expanded to include new ideas.

Small details need not appear in the outline, but an effective outline will show:

1. The **order** of the parts.
2. The **divisions** of the subjects.
3. The **relationships** of the parts.

III. THE FORM

A. Use **Roman** numerals (I,II) to indicate the **major** divisions.

B. Use **capital** letters (A,B) to indicate the **second** level of division.

C. Use **Arabic** numerals (1,2) to indicate the **third** level of division.

D. Use **lower-case** letters (a,b) to indicate the **fourth** level of division.

E. Use **Arabic** numerals within **parentheses** to indicate the **fifth** level of division.

F. Use a **period** after each number of letter.

G. **Indent** each subdivision approximately five spaces.

I._____

    A._____

    B._____

        1._____

        2._____

    C._____

II._____

    A._____

        1._____

            a._____

182

b._____

    2._____

B._____

    1._____

    2._____

    3._____

Complete the following:

(1)   An outline is a system of grouping ....facts.

(2)   With what signs are the main groups of an outline given?.........

(3)   Do all the details have to be included in the outline?...........

(4)   An effective outline will show:

    The ....of the parts.

    The division of the...........

    The............... of the parts.

IV.   THE DIVISION

The process of outlining is based on two principles of division.

A.   PRINCIPLE #1

1.   Make certain the outline covers the subject completely.
2.   The sum of the major headings must represent the entire subject.
3.   The sum of the subdivision must represent the entire major headings.

B.   PRINCIPLE #2

1.   Do not allow single headings to appear in the outline.
2.   The very fact of dividing implies two or more parts. This fact means if you have a I, you must have a II; if you have an A, you must have a B, etc.

Below is an outline. Read it carefully and notice the way the topics are listed.

The Care of a Pleasure Horse

I.   The Importance of Proper Care

II.   Proper Feeding
    A.   Amount and kinds of grain
    B.   Amount and kinds of hay
    C.   Fresh clean water

III.   Proper Grooming
    A.   Brushing and combing
    B.   Bathing
    C.   Health care
    D.   Clean stable

IV.   Proper Equipment
    A.   Bridles
    B.   Bits
    C.   Saddles

V.   A Healthy and Enjoyable Horse

Using the above outline as a guide, complete these equations:

1.   I (The Importance of Proper Care) + II + III + IV + V=_____

_____

2.   _____ + _____ + _____ = Proper Equipment.

V.   THE ARRANGEMENT

After you have decided on the major divisions on your subject (I, II, III, etc.) arrange the parts logically. The nature of the subject will usually suggest an appropriate arrangement.

The most common arrangements are:

    A.   There is a TIME pattern.

        1.   The main points are in chronological division.
        2.   The order progresses from a given point in time backward or forward.

    B.   There is a SPACE pattern.

        1.   The main points are determined by physical placement.
        2.   The order is from east to west, north to south, top to bottom, etc.

    C.   There is a CATEGORICAL pattern.

        1.   The main points are determined by a systematic classification based upon the relationship of the parts to the whole.

        2.   The order may follow one of several patterns:

            a.   the most important or interesting first and last with the least important in the middle.

            b.   the simple to the complex, or

        c. the familiar to the unfamiliar.

D. There is the CAUSE-EFFECT or EFFECT-CAUSE pattern.

   1. The main points are built around (I) the cause and (II) the effect.

   2. The order depends on whether you are seeking to determine the causes from the known effect or the effect from the known causes.

E. There is a PROBLEM-SOLUTION pattern.

   1. The main points are (I) the problem and (II) the solution.

   2. The order is obvious.

F. There is the REASONS-FOR or REASONS-AGAINST pattern.

   1. The main points are reasons for supporting or opposing a proposition.

   2. The order may be several of the above.

Make certain that the subheads in a section coordinate to each other and subordinate to the major headings.

WRONG: I.   The eighteenth century

          II.   The American Revolutionary War.

          Section II should be a subhead of Section I.

Use parallel structure for parallel parts of the outline.

WRONG: I.   Preparation of Soil (phrase).

          II.   Seeds (noun).

          How would you change the two points directly above to make them parallel?

SAMPLE OUTLINE OF THE GOSPEL OF MATTHEW

I. **The King - His Humanity.**

    A.   His Pedigree. 1:1-17
    B.   His Birth. 1:18-25
    C.   His Infancy. 2:1-23
    D.   His Baptism. 3:1-17
    E.   His Temptation. 4:1-11
    F.   His Ministry Begins.

II. **The Kingdom.**

    A.   The King's Citizens.
        1.   Character - 5:1-12
        2.   Influence - 5:13-16
    B.   The King's Laws.
        1.   Man's relation to man. 5:21-48. As to murder, adultery, divorce, oaths, revenge, enemies.
        2.   Man's relation to God. 6:1-34. As to alms, prayer, fasting, money, food, raiment, and judgement.
            a.   Spiritual - 6:1-18
            b.   Temporal - 6:19-34
    C.   Evidence of being in the Kingdom. 7:7-29. Two ways. Two Trees. Two Builders.

III. **The King's Ministry.**

    A.   His Deity and Humanity.

    B.   By His power
        1.   over disease. 8:1-22
        2.   over Nature. 8:23-27
        3.   over demons. 8:28-34
        4.   over sin. 9:1-8
        5.   over death. 9:18-26
        6.   over bodily affliction. 9:27-31

    C.   The King calls and commissions the Twelve. 9:36-38, 10:1-42

    D.   The King's witness of John the Baptist. 11:1-19

    E.   The King Upbraids cities of unbelief. 11:20-30

    F.   The King and the Sabbath Day. 12:1-13

    G.   The King and His only sign. 12:14-50

IV. **The Kingdom in Mystery Form.**

    A.   The Sower. 13:1-23

B. The Wheat and Tares. 13:24-30, 36-43

C. The Mustard Seed. 13:31-32

D. The Leaven and Meal. 13:33

E. The Hid Treasure. 13:44

F. The Pearl of Great Price. 13:45-46

G. The Dragnet. 13:47-58

H. The Scribe and the Kingdom of Heaven. 13:58

V. The King's Ministry Continued.

A. Death of the King's Forerunner. 14:1-13

B. The King Feeds 5000. 14:14-21

C. The King walks on the sea. 14:22-36

D. The King rebukes Scribes and Pharisees. 15:1-20

E. The King heals a Gentile. 15:21-28

F. The King feeds 4000. 15:29-39

G. The King and the Pharisees and Sadducees. 16:1-12

H. The King reveals the Church. 16:13-18, 19-20 The King, The Cross, the Glory to follow. 16:21-28

VI. The King In His Kingdom Glory.

A. The Transfiguration of the King. 17:1-27

B. The Kingdom in manifestation typically.

C. The King heals a Lunatic, 17:14-21

D. The King and His Cross. 17:22-23

E. The King and Temple Tax. 17:24-27.

VII. The King and His Teaching.

A. The Unmerciful Servant. 18:1-14, 15-35.

B. As to Marriage and Divorce. 19:1-12.

C. As to Children. 19:13-15.

D.   As to Riches. 19:16-26

E.   As to Vineyard Laborers. 19:17-20; 1-28.

VIII.   The King In Jerusalem.

    A.   The King's Journey to Jerusalem. 20:29-34

    B.   The King's Triumphant Entry. 21:1-11

    C.   The King in His Father's Temple. 21:12-17.

    D.   The King's Enemies. 21:18-23:33

    E.   The King's Parable of the Marriage Feast. 22:1-14

    F.   The King Farewell's the City in Warning. 23:33-39

IX.   The King as Prophet and Judge.

    A.   The King in Olivet. 24:1-51

    B.   The King's Parables.
          1.   The Ten Virgins 25:1-13
          2.   The Talents 25:14-30

    C.   The King and His Throne of Glory. 25:31-46.

X.   The King Rejected and Crucified.

    A.   The King Anointed for Burial. 26:1-13.

    B.   The King Eats the Passover. 26:17-35

    C.   The King in Gethsemane. 26:36-46

    D.   The King Betrayed and Arrested. 26:47-56.

    E.   The King on Trial. 26:57-27:14

    F.   The King Condemned. 27:15-26

    G.   The King Crucified. 27:27-56

    H.   The King Buried. 27:57-66

XI.   The King In Resurrection Glory.

    A.   The King Resurrected and Witnessed. 28:1-15

    B.   The King's Enemies deny the Resurrection.

XII. The King's Commission, and Ascension.

    A.   The King in the Appointed Mount. 28:16

    B.   The King commissions His Disciples. 28:17-20

    C.   The King Ascends until the Second Coming.

assignment #1

Below is a list of the main points and smaller points of an outline. Re-copy the items in the proper outline form, placing the points in the proper order. Be sure to indent each new division of points and keep the similar points with the same numbers or letters in a straight column. Pay attention to the way the points are related:

Living the Christian Life

A.   Respect parents

C.   Study as unto the Lord

II.   At home

I.   The importance of a good Christian life

A.   Respect the teacher

C.   Be involved in Christian ministries

III.   At school

B.   Speak to everyone and smile after the meeting

B.   Respect other students

A.   Pay attention to the minister

IV.   At church

B.   Be kind to brothers and sisters

C.   Help with chores willingly

V.   Following Christ

Living the Christian Life

OUTLINING WORKSHOP

assignment #2
Using the information on the preceding pages, fill in the spaces below with the data provided.

The Life of Christ

I._____

    A._____

    B._____

        1._____

        2._____

II._____

    A._____

    B._____

III._____

IV._____

    A._____

        1._____

        2._____

    B._____

    C._____

V._____

    A._____

    B._____

        1._____

        2._____

        3._____

    C._____

    D._____

VI._____

    A._____

    B._____

    C._____

Flight to Egypt
Visit to Jerusalem at 12
Before Pilate
Feeding the 5,000
Before Herod
Healing the sick
Laws of the Kingdom
Passion Week
Sermon on the Mount

Beatitudes
Early Life
Presentation of gifts
Post-Resurrection Events
Guiding star
Appearance to the Twelve
Visit of wise men
Before high priest
Forty days of preaching
Concerning Kingdom

Jesus on trial
Birth
Ascension
Burial
Crucifixion
Baptism
Triumphal entry
Visit of shepherds
Ministry

OUTLINING WORKSHOP

assignment #3

1.　　Make a full sentence outline of Matthew Chapter 23 using the following framework:

Title of the Chapter_____

I._____vs. 1-12

　　A._____vs. 1-10

　　　　1._____vs. 1-4

　　　　2._____vs. 5-10

　　　　　　a._____vs. 5a

　　　　　　b._____vs. 5b

　　　　　　c._____vs. 6a

　　　　　　d._____vs. 6b

　　　　　　e._____vs. 7-10

　　　　　　　　(1)_____vs. 7

　　　　　　　　(2)_____vs. 8-10

　　　　　　　　　　(a)_____vs. 8

　　　　　　　　　　(b)_____vs. 9

　　　　　　　　　　(c)_____vs. 10

　　B._____vs. 11-12

　　　　1._____vs. 12a

　　　　2._____vs. 12b

II._____vs. 13-36

　　A._____vs. 13

　　　　1._____vs. 13b

　　　　2._____vs. 13c

　　B._____vs. 14

　　　　1._____vs. 14b

　　　　2._____vs. 14c

　　　　3._____vs. 14d

　　C._____vs. 15

　　　　1._____vs. 15b

　　　　2._____vs. 15c

D._____vs. 16-22

    1._____vs. 16b-17

    2._____vs. 18-20

    3._____vs. 21-22

E._____vs. 23-24

    1._____vs. 23

    2._____vs. 24

F._____vs. 25-26

    1._____vs. 25

    2._____vs. 26

G._____vs. 27-28

    1._____vs. 27

    2._____vs. 28

H._____vs. 29-36

    1._____vs. 29-30

        a._____vs. 31

        b._____vs. 32

        c._____vs. 33

        d._____vs. 34

            (1)_____vs. 34b

            (2)_____vs. 34c

        e._____vs. 35

            (1)_____vs. 35b

            (2)_____vs. 35c

        f._____vs. 36

III._____vs. 37-39

  A._____vs. 37

  B._____vs. 38-39

    1._____vs. 38

    2._____vs. 39

194

Recommended Books with Bible Subject Outlines

600 BIBLE GEMS & OUTLINES
S.R. Briggs & John H. Elliott (Kregel)

1000 BIBLE STUDY OUTLINES
F.R. Marsh (Kregel)

Other Resources Available by Ken Malmin

Ken Malmin & Kevin J. Conner

The Covenants

Interpreting the Scriptures

New Testament Survey

Old Testament Survey

Ask for these resources at your local Christian bookstore.

City Christian Publishing
9200 NE Fremont
Portland OR 97220
503-253-9020
1-800-777-6057
www.CityChristianPublishing.com

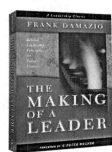
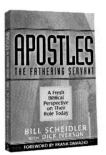
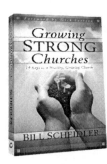

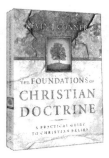

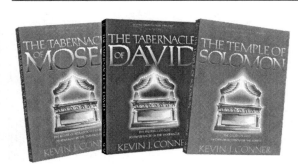

CPSIA information can be obtained
at www.ICGtesting.com
Printed in the USA
FFOW05n1139260716